Sexless

Sexless M

Sexless Marriage ane

By

Jay Stanbury

# Table of Contents

# Introduction

What is a sexless marriage? There are many descriptions out there but for this book, any marriage that has less than ten sexual encounters per year is a sexless marriage. There are also all kinds of numbers floating around in cyberspace that try to define how many sexless marriages there are. Some statistics say as many as forty million people in the North America live in sexless marriages others place the number somewhat lower. The certainty is that no one can know how many marriages have gone sexless but from what can be determined from therapists and surveys and other sources of information the numbers are staggering, well into the millions. As you can see, this has become a huge problem for many of the people involved and looks to be a driving force behind many divorces.

You may be thinking, well old people don't have sex anymore so that would account for a big portion of that number but it's just not true. There are newlyweds in sexless marriages with some that never get the marriage consummated. There are many people in all age groups dealing with this problem. The numbers seem to be growing along with a level of dissatisfaction that often results in affairs, divorces and other solutions to the problem.

It's not an exclusively male or female problem. Most people seem to think that men are always ready for sex and that they would never turn down sex if it were offered. This is patently untrue there are many women out there that can vouch for this. Many men are also married to women that will never engage in sexual contact under any circumstances. This sad state of affairs has become quite common and sadly it is robbing people of much of the joy that being married can provide to a couple that has a solid intimate relationship. This problem is not confined to marriages either it has also shown up in long-term relationships with same sex partners as well.

If two people that have a very low or no sex drive are married to each other, then it's pretty much a non-problem because they are in a relationship that is acceptable to them. The trouble starts when you have partners that are mismatched. Almost every person that gets married expects to have an intimate sexual relationship with his or her new spouse. According to the numbers, there are many people that have been disappointed; millions of them are living in sexless marriages. For some, it starts out bad but for others, it fades out over time but whichever way it happens it can still be painful.

It seems that sexless marriages are something that's kept secret because of the embarrassment factor, in our society the idea that someone will divorce their partner just because they have no sex life doesn't get much support. These marriages also lack intimacy and communications as well as other things that are essential for a good partnership. Dealing with people with "issues" eventually wears even the toughest person down. Whether it is a psychological problem or residue from past relationships or whatever it is will devastate the partnership because it eventually winds up with one partner making a unilateral decision that there will be no more sex without bothering to consult the other person. No one has the right to make that decision for someone else, and anyone that does that has essentially declared that their participation in their marriage is over.

This book is written from the refused spouse's perspective – it will not go into detail as to how to fix a sexless/celibate marriage, as from gathered research, forums and written articles it is nigh on impossible to turn the situation around to a relationship where both partners are having their needs met. Rather it will talk about what you can discuss and try in order to realize and act upon choices, if you cannot continue living in such a relationship.

# Chapter 1.  Sexless Marriage

In some relationships, there is no sex before marriage. The couple gets married, and at that point, one partner has already decided that there will be no sex in the relationship, this almost always occurs without any consultation with their partner. Frequently this results in an annulment of the marriage or a very rapid divorce. This is the worst sort of mismatch and is usually so obvious that it will be corrected quickly. Sometimes people will stay in these relationships because they feel compelled by religion or family pressures to avoid divorce.

In most places if the marriage never results in sex then it can usually be annulled easily. Most religions also recognize this as a valid reason to terminate the marriage. An annulment restores you to unmarried status as if the marriage never happened.

Another kind of sexless marriage is the marriage that starts out with an acceptable level of sex for both partners but somewhere along the way one partner withdraws from sexual contact. It might happen at any time during the marriage. There seem to be some events that can happen in the marriage that can act as triggers for this behavior. Some of them are: having children, high levels of stress, an affair by one partner, physical illness, depression, loss of a job, mental illness and there are many others because this problem is often a combination of things. In some instances, this turns out to be temporary and after a time sex returns but in many cases, this is the end. This seems to be the most popular situation, and it can affect any marriage of any length.

Sadly this problem seldom resolves itself in a way that allows the rebuilding of a relationship. The people that need an intimate relationship often tolerate these circumstances for years before they finally resolve that enough is enough and leave for greener pastures. Many of them have affairs looking for intimacy or attempting to restore their self-confidence. Some people will just find other things that keep them occupied such as friends, hobbies and other activities but many times it comes down to divorce.

Separating people into groups like refusers (this is the term used to describe those who will not participate in the married sexual relationship) and people that want intimate relationships is very simplistic, and there is a lot of a gray area that falls somewhere in between. It seems that the relationship becomes more of a battle than anything positive. After so much ill will has been built up over time there is seldom any way to get back to a place where love is even possible anymore. There is too much anger and resentment which are like sowing the fields with salt because once that is done there is no retrieving the situation and the only logical thing to do would be to go your separate directions. Since when have people ever done the logical thing though, many people have hung on for decades in dead relationships for their reasons. It wears a person down though, and eventually, something has to break somewhere just to relieve the stress.

There are tons of books on the market that claim to be able to solve these problems but if they could do it wouldn't the millions of people that are in sexless marriages have all read the book and fixed the problem by now? There is no claim in this book that a sexless marriage can be fixed because statistically, the success rate for turning this problem around is pretty dismal. This book is an exploration of the reasons behind sexless marriage and is designed to shed light into some of the areas that sometimes get ignored. It is also aimed at helping you determine what your response to your situation will be. This is a smorgasbord of information that will allow you to pick among different items to help you understand your situation and hopefully eventually find your answer.

My qualifications to write this book include living in a sexless marriage, going through a divorce, multiple college degrees, and many years as a teacher dealing with families of all sorts, and reading through mountains of research and various publications. My goal is to distil what I've learned and read into something ordinary people can understand and use to figure out their situations.
Statistics will be kept to a minimum because for the individual they have little meaning and most of them about sexless marriages from what I can determine are simply guesses. If you are reading this it's not because you are doing research on sexless marriage, it's more likely that you are trying to understand your situation and figure out some way to cope with it.

Living in a sexless marriage can be a very lonely experience, and far too many people have no idea that they are part of a large group. They often feel alone and sometimes even ashamed because they somehow get the idea that a sexless marriage is their fault, that they must have done something to cause the rejection they are getting. But lesson number one is that feeling that way is the wrong answer because you aren't asking the right questions.

Consider who in the marriage is denying their partner sex. This person in the jargon of the sexless marriage community is known as a REFUSER. As long as you have one person in the supposed relationship who fails to engage you have a seriously flawed relationship this can also be an abusive relationship. Consider the mental anguish of the person who is being constantly rejected by their spouse this sort of treatment is a form of abuse. In the past, this was considered to be grounds for divorce, and at that time it was known as mental cruelty. Things have changed now, and in most places, there is simply no requirement to prove anything to get a divorce. We have become a society of throw away relationships. If you don't like the one you have you simply toss it on the trash heap and get another. Serial marriage has become so common now that many kids have multiple step-parents before they even graduate from High School.

Society has changed a great deal since the days of our grandparents in those days divorce was a rarity and almost always came at the end of long periods of physical abuse or was the result of someone having an affair and getting caught red handed. But even then many people patched things up and continued often claiming it was for the sake of the children this resulted in many bitter and angry people living together and guessed what happened to their children when they grew up and tried to establish their relationships.

Our ability to interact with each other has been slipping for quite a while since schools have turned more or less into prison type environments where interaction between kids is constantly discouraged, and we are paying a big price for those to sit down and shut up rules. Children no longer get much experience dealing with others, making friendships or interacting which once gave them some basis for guiding their behavior. Technology has turned children into loners who seldom talk to each other face to face. It's no surprise really that the divorce rate for new marriages these days hovers at around 53% within the first eight years. It's monkey see, and monkey does too as the damage field of our inability to communicate grows exponentially with each new generation. We are crippling ourselves emotionally and causing people to be withdrawn by encouraging children to stay away from each other in school and enforcing the sit down shut up and don't talk type of rules that are so popular these days in the schools (penal institutions).

In some places we still have values and manners do still exist but it is becoming the exception rather than the rule, and we are paying the price for this. In smaller towns where people tend to have more community and the schools still retain some of the flavors of days gone by more kids do learn manners. At least to some degree and those who attend church regularly tend to be even more polite and less me-centered than in more urban environments. The cities are filled with gang members and thugs, and kids now will tell you they plan on growing up to be pimps and hoes because that has been glamorized. Our narcissistic and self- centered children in some ways don't even notice that other people even exist because they have become so wrapped up in themselves that they can only form groups with others similar to themselves and the result is a total disassociation with community or society in general. This is coming home to roost with a vengeance as we see stupidity carried to extremes as people riot over nonexistent causes and use that pretense for destroying everything around them. We have created mindless golems of destruction instead of citizens who value anything, and we are paying the price for that as they seek to live without and effort or ambition on their part.

We have created monsters that do not care about anything but themselves and their immediate gratification. What expectation could we possibly have that these narcissistic infants could ever grow up to be responsible citizens capable of loving relationships and be worthy of anything at all?

# Chapter 2.  Reasons For A Sexless Marriage

There are several reasons why a couple might fall into a sexless marriage. Often it's not a simple case of the two getting bored of each other, or of them not being best for each other in the first place. In fact, there are many complex and nuanced reasons why a marriage that was fruitful in the beginning might have become fallow and sexless after some time.

The list below is incomplete, of course, since no list could ever cover all the possible reasons for a sexless marriage. It's worth a look though, as a starting point for considering the things that might be contributing to your sexless marriage. For the time being, give all these reasons equal consideration, and think seriously about whether or not they could apply to you.

## Medical Issues

There are a huge variety of medical issues that can interrupt a healthy sex life. Some are physical, and some are mental, but all can be equally disruptive. Medical conditions can arise out of nowhere and can affect people who have always been otherwise perfectly healthy. For men, this can take the form of impotence, pain, a lack of interest in sex, or a complex with regards to sexual acts. For women, vaginal pain is a common occurrence, as are issues relating to sex or a sudden decline in sexual interest.

If you think that the cause of your sexless marriage is medical in nature, it's important to get help from a trained professional. It may seem embarrassing to take such personal problems to your doctor, but it's important to remember that they will have seen it all a hundred times before. They are the best qualified to help, too, and will provide far better advice (and therapy or medication if necessary) than you can get from your friends, family or the internet.

It's worth considering medical issues, even if you've seen no sign that this might be the case. An abrupt an unexplained change in attitude or mental state can sometimes have a medical cause, and in the case of your partner, it may be that they're hiding a medical issue that they don't wish to discuss with you or even admit to having. Do your very best not to leave any medical issue untreated, as untreated conditions are almost guaranteed to worsen over time.

Bear in mind also that a lack of sexual interest can be caused by medication just as much as an illness can cause it. If you or your partner have started taking any new medication recently, make sure to either consult your doctor about it or read up on the possible side effects. Often if a drug or medication is having a negative effect on your sex life, it is possible to find an alternative treatment – make sure to make your concerns known to your physician though, and don't just suffer in silence.

## Stress

Stress can be an absolute killer when it comes to libido. When stressed by issues outside of the marriage, it can be difficult to find the right energy to get involved in sexual activity. Some people find it impossible to switch off when something is bothering them. Instead of being in the moment with their partner, they are instead distracted; constantly worrying about the thing that's stressing them.
It can be difficult to realize sometimes when you or your partner are under stress, as there is a tendency to become so focused on whatever is stressing you that the effects of the stress become barely noticeable by comparison.

Take a moment to evaluate the stresses and strains in your life and consider whether any of them might be troubling you so much that it is having an impact on your sex life. Economic problems, children and family commitments, and issues at work are some of the most common causes of stress in the modern world. If your partner is likely to be experiencing any of these issues make sure to give them space, as well as the opportunity to talk about the troubles they're having. The power of being able to talk about your stresses should not be underestimated.

## Tiredness

This is another incredibly common factor in sexless marriages. Sex and intimacy both require an abundance of energy and if either you or your partner are exhausted then that energy can be nearly impossible to come by. It is a well-known fact that we as a society are getting less sleep than ever before, and less time to rest and recuperate as well. If your life has become more hectic, or if you struggle to get sufficient quality sleep and rest on a regular basis, consider whether this might be impacting on your sex life.

It's also worth stating one of the most common causes of tiredness that affects married couples: children. In the early years of their life, kids don't stick to a set sleeping pattern and can wake up at any hour of the night or day. They require constant attention and feeding, and they can result in a lot less sleep for the mother and father. If you have just had a child, you should expect the lack of sleep to result in a dip in your sex life!

## Lack Of Excitement

In the early days of almost any relationship, sex is usually a pretty common occurrence. When you meet someone new, you are naturally excited about them – after all, there's plenty still to discover. Their pleasures and proclivities are all unknown to you and represent new territory to be explored. By the time you get married, however, you usually know someone pretty well.

Married couples have less new territory to explore, and so their married sex life can seem unexciting compared to how it used to be. Often they find what they both enjoy early on, and settle into a kind of sexual routine. Though they may both find this satisfying, the routine is hardly likely to be exciting, and they may find that they are less than enthusiastic about it after a while.

Variety and excitement are more important to us as humans than many of us realize. We need constantly changing stimulation to keep us alive, awake and on our toes. If there's nothing new to be discovered or experienced, we quickly begin to lose interest in sex and intimacy. For this reason, it's important to keep your sex life varied and interesting, by trying out new things or revisiting old ones. Take a moment to consider whether you've fallen into a sexual routine, and think about ways in which you might be able to break out of it.

## An Affair

Although it's important not to be too paranoid, and not to inherently mistrust your partner, an affair is also the cause behind a large number of sexless marriages. There are many reasons why an affair might cause a marriage to become sexless – and the most obvious one is that it is indicative of other problems elsewhere. If communication between a married couples has broken down to the point that one of them feels the need to look elsewhere for sexual fulfillment, then naturally the sex between the married couple is going to suffer as well. Conversely, an affair can result from a sexless marriage – with the unfulfilled partner "outsourcing" to get their needs met.

There's also the fact that every individual only has a limited amount of sexual energy to give – this is particularly the case for men. If the vast majority of sexual energy, attention, and excitement is expended elsewhere, then there will be little left over to spare for the marriage. This can lead to a lack of interest in maintaining the marriage and a lack of interest in sex in general.

Finally, it's also possible that when having an affair an individual may find more excitement in the person with whom they are having an affair than they will with their spouse. The person with whom they are having an affair is, after all, new and different – whereas their marriage is something that they've always had, and that they perhaps think they always will. It is difficult to find a marriage exciting when there is something else newer and more varied on offer. Not only that, but the act of having an affair can also be exciting in and of itself – secrets can be very stimulating. For all these reasons an affair can interfere with marriage, and cause it to become sexless. While it shouldn't be your first conclusion that your partner is having an affair, it should be something that you think about, and perhaps even something that you discuss.

## An Unresolved Argument

Just as an affair can disrupt the sex life within a marriage, so too can a fight, argument or disagreement that goes unresolved. The tension and negative energy from unresolved issues tend to linger and can prove to be a massive distraction from sex. If two people don't feel entirely comfortable with each other, it's unlikely that they'll be able to relax and let themselves go enough to have fulfilling sex with one another.

For this reason, it's important to make sure that you always resolve fights and arguments as soon as possible. This can often mean having unpleasant and difficult discussions – discussions that you'd much rather avoid altogether, but ones that are truly necessary for the health and well-being of your relationship. Do your best to be open and giving in the way that you communicate with your partner, and make sure that they do the same. In this way, you can be tackled problems as they arise, and not allow them to fester and become the cause of sexless in your relationship.
It may also be that you're unaware of the unresolved tension or disagreement that's causing friction between you and your partner.

Take a moment to think back, and consider whether there are any major or difficult differences between you. This can be a useful thing to discuss with your partner as well – often there can be something subconscious which is bothering one or both partners, the nature of which cannot be identified until it is spoken about.

# Chapter 3. Relationships Today

If you were to look at the statistics, you would have to conclude that intimate relationships and marriages are in serious trouble. Western societies have a divorce rate that is well over fifty percent. And that's just for first marriages; the stats don't include other committed relationships. For couples in their second and third marriages, it's even worse, with the percentage of divorces climbing to nearly seventy-five percent. It's clear that things are simply not working and the havoc reeked upon most people from the failure of their marriage or relationship is profound. Divorce is the biggest single factor in determining your wealth level. And think about the emotional turmoil; the courts today are filled with couples acrimoniously battling over their breakup, often involving bitter rows over the children.

For couples who stay in a marriage, things aren't much better. The "Sexless Marriage" (defined as where a couple has sex fewer than ten times a year) is turning into an epidemic, and it's estimated that up to 30% of marriages in this category. This is not only astounding, but it is also absolutely tragic.

So it's clear that things aren't working. But why is this case? After all, it was not so long ago that marriage seemed a safe and holy institution. And no couple goes into a marriage expecting it to fail.
There are many reasons for the high numbers of relationship breakdowns.

Firstly, our expectations for our relationships are much higher these days than they have been in earlier generations. This is positive. We as a community have largely moved on from focusing on mere survival to wanting fulfillment and deeper happiness in our lives. And we want more and better sex (and so we should).
Going back just one or two generations, we find that marriage had quite a different purpose to today. Marriage existed to serve two primary functions:

## Survival
In a harsh world, our chances of survival were much greater when we had a partner. It meant we could share our resources, responsibilities, and skills and watch out for each others safety. Should we die (through the common

hazards of war, accidents, and disease) our children would also have another to provide the necessary care?

## Reproduction

The survival of the species was enhanced by the sexual union and nurturing of the offspring that a marriage partnership allowed.
So marriage developed as the ideal framework to achieve the goals of the wider community.

Society today is of course radically different. With the developments in technology, concern for where the next meal is coming from it is something few of us spend much time worrying about. There are no wild animals or hostile tribes wandering about wanting to cause us harm. The drastic reduction in the mortality rate means that we needn't fear our children are not going to survive past infancy.
We all have much more time and security to be able to focus on meeting our higher needs, such as our overall happiness, realizing our potential and achieving individual fulfillment.

Of course, with relationships being such a central part of this, we want a lot more from this aspect of our lives as well. We don't need someone to help put food on the table; we want someone to help meet our emotional and sexual needs. And if they don't (and of course this is much more difficult than simply helping us survive) it creates difficulties; we are faced with the choice of either accepting the situation or of moving on to find someone else.

In earlier generations, the roles and expectations within a relationship were defined. Even in our parents' day, Dad went out to work, and mom stayed at home to rear the children and maintain the home. This clarity provided its security. It is debatable whether or not people were happier, but they were certainly more settled.
Even counseling and traditional therapy still tend to operate using tools that aren't suited to our 21st Century lifestyles and expectations.

With more emphasis on individual fulfillment, relationships are nothing like that today. There is a much greater freedom to explore who we are, without the restrictions of gender or financial status. Everything is a lot more complicated, and there is no longer anything that can be classed as being 'typical.'

One of the problems that have arisen, as far as relationships are concerned, is that traditional therapy and counseling has failed to keep pace. The simple tools of the past no longer work. It is hardly any wonder that an estimated 70% of counseling is ineffective in helping couples resolve their problems. The result is that most people are simply not getting what they want from their relationship. Relationships can become a descending spiral of unhappiness: as things deteriorate, we tend to put in less effort and focus. This only makes things worse.

We're bombarded with media images of wonderfully happy and sexually excitingly passionate relationships, but when that doesn't happen for us, we just accept it as "the way things are in real life" and put our efforts into things other than our relationship.

The problem is that we can never be truly happy without a deeply fulfilling relationship. Despite what you might want to think, there is nothing that will have more of an impact on the quality of your happiness than the quality of your relationship. You can have everything else - money, fame, wonderful family and friends - but without a truly satisfying intimate relationship, there will always be something inside you that gnaws away at your heart. We simply can't get away from the fact that as human beings we are wired for sexual intimacy. And the only thing that can give us that is a loving partner!

## Defining The Problem

It's not that the refusers are bad or evil people for the most part; the problem is that they are just totally incompatible with someone that wants an intimate and sexually vibrant lifestyle. Being friends is about the best you can ever be with these people because lovers they are not and never will be. Convincing ourselves that we have made a bad investment and that we must move on can be a Herculean task because we are stubborn, and most of us are convinced that we can fix things but there is no fixing this and besides we don't have the right to expect someone else to change to meet our expectations. We are who we are, and they are who they are and if there is no common ground where love can grow you are wasting your life.

We are who we are, and there seem to be at least two distinct types of people. Those who need a lot of interaction with other people and those who are perfectly happy with themselves (actually I think they are lying, probably even to themselves). Even as babies some people require more momma face time and attention than others do so perhaps this is something we may be born into. The disastrous problem occurs when two opposites hook up.

Most healthy people can enjoy the physical stimulation of sex. It feels good enough that while in courtship mode we can all manage to get the deed done. Even in that mode, there is some attraction, and there is enough interaction to set off our bodies response which is hormonal and makes us a little looney tunes for a while. So usually the initial stages of courtship behavior are fairly similar for most people. Our hormones often have a big effect on our attitude and desire for the other person that we are engaging in sex with. Unfortunately, most of this will pass because this is Nature's way to get us to reproduce.

We often forget that we share characteristics with the animal kingdom simply because we never think of ourselves as animals. But we share some of the same instincts and biological imperatives that our animal kingdom has. Hormones have a lot of impact on our behaviors, and yet we always seem to think we are in control of it all. We are at war in a sense between what our physical bodies want and what our minds seem to feel is more appropriate. We rely heavily on learned behaviors to make us "socially acceptable" but unfortunately a goodly number of our fellows never got the memo, and some of those behaviors just don't seem to be working as planned.

Often we fool ourselves assuming that the physical lust we feel is the love we will need for a long term relationship. These relationships that we engage in have metamorphosed through time from an economically driven partnership which was often arranged by parents to expand the influence and wealth of the "family." Until recently in history life was difficult and mere survival was often a struggle so getting a good strong partner was critical. Bringing someone into the "family" who could bring resources was extremely beneficial. There was a song by Tina Turner titled "What's Love Got To Do With It, " and in bygone days the answer to that question was very little indeed.

Our modern concept of relationships and "love" has developed as life became easier and there was less stress in the effort to live and thrive. We like to think of ourselves as rational, civilized beings but this is a very thin veneer under which lie behaviors we have inherited from a more primitive past. Those hormone things have awesome power when they are unleashed they can cause us to behave in ways foreign to our normal mode. It can make you feel fantastic or drag you to the depths of despair and what stinks is that you do not have control of this roller coaster once you climb aboard you are in for the ride. If we have learned what the effects are and if we have recognized what these chemicals can do to us thinking may still be possible.

One problem with our roller coaster is that we may be on the ride of our life while the other person involved is merely on the "kiddie coaster" this kind of mismatch often results in "broken hearts" which can put us in the dumpster emotionally. This too can be a side effect of the "hormone chemistry blitz." But there is another more insidious problem that can lie hidden and it is often brought about by what we consider to be social behavior, and we lie to ourselves.

This is the root of many sexless marriages that start out seeming what we consider "NORMAL" and this causes people to pair up because there is an assumption that things will "work out." But what this is could be called a mismatch because the motivations are skewed. One person may be anticipating a highly intimate relationship with lots of physical interaction while the other has little interest in this but is looking for someone to share the chores of life with. That is a sexless marriage waiting to happen, and it often will degenerate to this often after there are children born if it gets that far.

We are not perfect, and we are not robots that can be programmed and few people have iron control of their emotions. Many people don't even understand themselves and what they want especially when they are young and physically vigorous. We often mistake lust for love, and that can cost us more than we want to spend in pain and negative feelings. As we grow old most of us begin to understand ourselves better, we figure out what motivates us, and sometimes we are even able to get a grip on what we want out of life. Sadly we often look at the person that we paired up with when we were twenty something, and we discover that we don't know them at all. This is often termed as drifting apart, but the reality is that you were never together in the first place. You were two people on different tracks that ran parallel for a distance then diverged.

It takes fortitude and courage to create a solid long term relationship it requires compassion willingness to sacrifice and courage; you have to be willing to "get your hands dirty" and be in charge of creating the relationship to perpetuate it. At some point as we age the physical hormone driven life deserts us and then we must make a decision. Will we love or not? Can we stay with this person that we have bound ourselves too until our lives finish up? Or are we so empty of what we feel that we need that we must move on? Realize this is a decision that both of you must make and this determines whether the relationship will continue or die. This is where we find in our hearts whether we are capable of real love for each other after the lust has faded.

Sex at this point in a relationship becomes about giving because if you love you give to each other. By now you both should have a good idea of what it takes to please each other but love is what makes you put forth the effort. What you can gain from pleasing your partner it is an investment in your happiness as long as the effort is mutual. That is the key to it all there must be a mutual desire to please each other this is the sharing of a deep tie that is the glue that creates true and lasting love. Without this glue, a relationship can become a shell that has the appearance of being alive but lacks real substance. It has degenerated into a living arrangement for two people who have little in common and who are afraid to try anything else so they stay chained together but there is little happiness to be found.

Keeping love alive requires not only desire but conscious effort everything cannot be spontaneous and waiting for the "right moment" is simply foolish especially if you have kids. You have to engage not only your heart in a relationship, but you must keep your mind working on it too. But this often requires that you take turns at being the aggressor and the plaything which is a scenario that you can build in your imagination.

Oops! There I've let out a major secret a relationship requires imagination you need to be able to visualize what pleases your partner and then you must be willing to do it, and this must be a two-way street, and there must be some frequency. Once a year on your anniversary is not enough because what you are doing by pleasing each other is building the bond that makes a relationship work. You are saying in this way that I care about you and want you to be happy this is a concrete expression that says "You are important to me." This is something that words will never be able to express nearly as well as a crazy little romp under the covers where someone gets a little surprise pleasure.

Giving your partner pleasure is the expression of love and showing that you're involved in their life and that you care enough about their happiness to extend yourself on their behalf. But this can never work if it is one sided it must be mutual and it must be a high priority for both of you. But understand that pleasure is not always about sexual intimacy has many facets, giving someone a small unexpected gift just because or taking the time to do a little extra something special for someone is legitimate expressions of caring as well and should be part of the whole picture. What kills many relationships is when one partner gets a strong vibe that they are no longer important in the life of their partner when they start feeling neglected and taken for granted it's a short path to the door and out.

20

It's seriously about giving a damn about each other and your life together, and I know that can be hard with all the distractions available to us these days. Many people are constantly on the run doing all sorts of things except they aren't taking the time to do each other. Taking your partner for granted is surely poisonous to the basic relationship and that can cut both ways. People have become selfish and lazy these days since we have more "leisure time" than ever. The reality of what kills many relationships is simply neglect. People get used to having that other person around, and they get comfortable with having someone who does some of the chores required for living. But they forget what they promised each other when they married in the first place.

It's time for you to both lay your cards on the table, and the burning question that you must answer is "Do you still love each other"? I'm not talking about tolerating each other or being satisfied with the maintenance arrangements and the division of chores. What I'm talking about is do you still love that person across the table from you enough to get real with each other and quit ignoring what relationships are about. If you find that you cannot look at that person whom you should know pretty well by now and feel love and concern for their happiness then the reality is that there are two options you can either set up a living arrangement that allows survival but perhaps little mutual happiness or you can hit the quick release button and go back into the marketplace for someone who loves you as you feel you need to be loved. One alternative is painful the other is madness I'll let you figure out which is which but it shouldn't be hard at all.

# Chapter 4. The Masculine and Feminine

Women experience themselves and their world very, very differently to men. You cannot use your male brain and male way of thinking to understand women. Understanding women give you the knowledge and beliefs to act in ways that tap into her feminine psyche. It is deeper than what she merely wants; she needs it. If she does not get what she needs to feel like a woman she will never be happy being with you.

Why should you care? Well, when she is not getting what she needs there is no chance she will genuinely and deeply care about your happiness and what you want. However, while she feels there is still a flicker of hope, she will try– yet again - to do something caring for you or give you what she thinks you want. Please know, however; she is doing this because she hopes, more than anything, you will finally give her what she needs.

People often do for others what they would like another person to do for them. Knowing this, if she is acting overly attentive and close or organizing something special, it might be her warm, generous and loving nature, or it might be because she perceives a void and wants to receive what it is she is doing for you.

This book is not for people who are in relationships that are not right. This book is for characters who know they are with the right partner but are experiencing frustration and misunderstanding within that relationship.

There is one word that simply encapsulates what a woman wants to feel like her man. It is a word that describes the obvious. You may think that you and she have this in your relationship already. If you are having problems understanding her, then chances are high it is missing too often in your relationship. This word needs to be reinforced over and over and over again. It needs to be over and identifiable to her with obvious examples. It cannot be assumed to be there.

Women sift through the world differently to men. Remember that the masculine energy is about doing things, achieving and getting a sense of worth and fulfillment from having an influence in the external world. In a word, it is about respect. Men want to feel respected for their abilities, knowledge, and achievements.

Conversely, feminine energy is about passivity and receptivity. Women notice the world around them and the people within it to see how people are responding to them. This is how they get their sense of who they are and their worth. Their feeling of worth and achievement comes in relationship to other people. In a word, women want to feel loved.

No one is saying you have to change who you are. You don't have to change what is important to you to give a woman what she wants. No one is saying you have to emasculate yourself and put her on a pedestal. If she experiences you doing any of these things she will not only no longer be getting what she wants, but she will have lost hope that you are a man who can give her what she wants to feel.
There are moments throughout the day where the opportunity arises for you to be the man who she has chosen to make her feel how she wants to feel.

It is as simple as that. Women want a feeling, and the feeling they want is that you and she are together. She wants to feel that you are together, a team, connected, harmonious, supportive of each other, caring for each other's well-being, accepting, acknowledging and appreciating each other together.

You might sit and say but what about me? To say 'I want this and that, sex, no nagging, no moodiness and no clinginess before I can feel close, connected and together with her' is backward.
In fact, as I said above, in her mind she has likely done many things at times for you in the secret hope that you will switch on and realize what she wants to feel. Likely you have just interpreted her actions as her being nice, or that she wants to do those things for you, or heaven forbid you to think it is her job.

She does those things because she wants them done to her, by you! If not you then there will be another man, or woman, somewhere at some time, sooner or later who understands this simple secret and she will have no incentive, drive or desire to pursue together-ness with you anymore. Or, she might stick around for many years until the children are older, but she will be unhappy and disillusioned, and so will you.

Where else in the natural course of events does the feminine initiate action or movement? No, where that I notice. The flower doesn't come to the bee. The masculine energy gives and is active, and the feminine is passive and receives. It is only after receiving does the feminine give back willingly, easily and naturally with great passion and heart.

So to spell it out for you in detail, if you want your wife to be more loving, nurturing, caring, and interested in having sex with you then you need to fulfill her wants first. It is only when she feels fulfilled, and she feels her femininity in relationship to your masculine energy will she be able to let those natural feminine tendencies express themselves.

You see, when the masculine gives the feminine what she desires than as a course of nature the masculine gets what he desires. Let nature takes its course, and everyone wins. Be selfish and act like an eight-year old who wants to receive but not give, or receive before giving, and you will both not get what you want. It just does not work when the masculine fails to provide the feminine a chance to feel desirable and attractive, not only physically, but as the whole woman that she is. By allowing her to feel special to at least one man in the universe, she will not feel alone. Instead, she will feel together as a team with you close and connected, cared about and loved.

It is likely you were completely unaware that it is that simple, or maybe you thought you were giving this to her but in reality, you are miles off the mark. Either be the same and selfish, or change and willingly play the part of the man. Be a man who expresses his masculine energy by acting in a way that allows a woman to feel her femininity. A man who loves women and loves the woman he is with and knows how to communicate that to her often will have everything he desires plus extra.

## As with dance, so it is with life.

We all have both feminine and masculine forces, but at certain times of the day she wants you to play the part of being the masculine energy, and she wants to experience the completeness of her feminine energy. Of course in a relationship, there are two people and two people need to work together to understand the other's values and fears, but the crucial point is without the man doing the man's part, the woman is stuck in a loop of frustration and compensation. She has to wait, or leave. How long will she wait? Who knows, but you can bet she won't be happy and there is no chance you will be either.

I recall a quote I heard 'women leave too soon and men leave too late.' This means that at the start of a relationship it is likely the women who decide it is not right quickly, maybe too quickly at times, and in a long-term relationship, it is the man who will tolerate and rarely bring a stagnant relationship to a head. The woman will initiate the end.

24

As a man it will be more tolerable to you than to her to be in a relationship that is not working. To a woman, she will only tolerate it for so long before she will without guilt have an affair or leave. You must understand that without a few certain feelings she will be driven by force greater than you are aware exists to seek these feelings elsewhere. If you are not going to be the man to provide the opportunity for her to feel these feelings, then she will choose someone else. This is a woman in her natural state. On our own, we can't feel the experience of connection with another, and this is a big part of what she needs. When you are the man that provides the feminine with what she needs to appear, then you feel fulfilled as a man.

Men like to feel powerful, clever, skilled and talented. Tapping into your natural masculine essence you get the power and freedom to give women what they want to feel, and then you get to feel how you want to feel. Good luck if you think that a woman should act in ways that allow you to feel everything you want to feel if you haven't done anything to look after the way she wants to feel. How she wants to feel is cared for, understood and together with confident, mature masculine energy.

# Chapter 5.  Sex And Physical Fitness

Let's face it a whole bunch of people out there so physically unfit that having sex is pretty much out of the question. On the other hand, there are probably even more who are not fit enough to enjoy sex if they do manage to get an offer. Oh sure there are all kinds of myths that obese people have sex and all that but this is the voice of reality talking if you are over 100 pounds overweight sex is more likely to be life threatening than enjoyable. I'm not saying that you cannot possibly have a sex life if you are obese and out of shape but what I am telling you is that if you shed some pounds and get your lungs and heart in shape, you will enjoy sex more. Some people are just all about themselves when it comes to sex, and their only concern is their orgasm. This kind of jackass makes a very poor partner because they not only don't share they seldom even care if their partner is getting anything from the "so called" relationship.

So if you don't have a reasonably good sex life and want one, then you need to get your sad butt in shape for it not only for yourself but your partner. Consider this how attracted would you be to your partner if they suddenly gained 100 pounds? You may still love them dearly as a person, but chances are they won't be all that attractive to you sexually. Good sex is a kind of athletic event that requires flexibility, strength and the ability to move you should also have enough stamina to survive the encounter. Many people who are complaining about their lack of a sex life aren't capable of participating in a strenuous sex session due to infirmity. But does that mean that they should be denied the bonding power of intimate expression? NO, it does not, but this also complicates things as things like erectile dysfunction and hypoactive sexual desire disorder start creating road blocks. Many men who experience erectile dysfunction are ashamed of this problem and will avoid sexual contact due to fear of failure.

Most Americans have gone soft from an easy lifestyle of sitting on the couch too much overeating junk instead of real food and just doing nothing. There are exceptions to every rule and this is not universal there are still some active, vital people out there who exercise regularly and who eat healthy food and who have magnificent sex lives. Those people are the exemption to the rule and not what the general public tends to do. We need to make more active vital people, and that means that huge four letter word WORK no matter how we slice it and dice it sex takes work and to do that work your body needs to be prepared. I'm not saying that being a "Chunky Monkey" makes it impossible to have sex or enjoy it but I am saying that you need a certain level of fitness to both have sex and enjoy the experience. Let's face it a fit body just feels better and is more capable. But even more important than the state of your body is the state of your attitude. Sometimes love isn't easy and at times we may even detest our partners a little bit, but you signed on for the long haul so you need to work from a base of caring about your partner if you can no longer do this then you are wasting both your time and theirs. A long term relationship isn't for the faint of heart it takes stamina, a willingness to sacrifice for the relationship and something most people seem to be missing a gracious acceptance of what your partner gives you.

Many people think that the opposite of love would be hate, but I am more inclined to say that the opposite would be indifference which is much harder to deal with than active hatred. As people move into a long term relationship, it is easy to start taking things for granted and get into a routine. But allowing yourself to do those things will eventually cause your relationship to go stale. You may both become bored with each other and at that point alienation of affection sets in big time.

You may very well begin behaving more like roommates than as married people. There are tons of people out there living together more like roommates than as lovers it's an easy pattern to fall into, and it takes a committed pair to turn this around, but it can be done. But this kind of arrangement is not uncommon at all, and with so many sexless marriages this is for many the normal state of affairs. Getting fit has enormous benefits for your health and your attitude it will strengthen your body and improve your sense of well-being both of which are necessary for a good sex life. It takes a bit of determination to admit to yourself that you need to overhaul yourself a bit or even a lot and it will always be easier if you work together as a team.

There are tons of books and videos designed to help people learn about diet and exercise but many of these are fads, and often they are designed to sell you meal plans, supplements or some quack piece of gear that will supposedly turn you into a muscly hottie overnight. I have bad news for you they are junk, and they will not help you to change your habits of a lifetime. Yes, I understand that you may be very out of shape and possibly have a lot of weight to lose. For some people with serious problems with obesity, the Lap Band or even the Gastric Sleeve weight loss surgeries may be an option that you should explore.

For the average person who is getting a little creaky in the joints running is probably not a great option but swimming is great because it puts a little stress on your joints while it uses almost every muscle in your body. If you aren't a great swimmer try using a mask and snorkel which makes it easier to breathe and that way you can also use whatever kind of stroke works for you. Walking is also an excellent exercise as long as you walk at a brisk pace and get some serious distance and it can also be a companionable way to spend time together.

As for diet, there are tons of diet books but almost any diet will require you to become serious about cooking, and that is a good thing. Fast food is a killer full of chemicals and garbage your body doesn't need. The Atkins Diet which is a low carb type is effective, and the South Beach Diet is similar the more recent Paleo Diet which emphasizes fresh whole foods is also very effective. But the solution is that you need to build up a stock of recipes that you like and provide yourself with a variety of foods. One of the biggest reasons that people are overweight is that the do not eat healthy foods, and with the constant bombardment for Whoppers, Milkshakes, Sodas and all that other crap it's hard to resist something that is fast and easy and has more calories in it than you will burn off in a couple of days. Our society has made food into entertainment, and that has created a nightmare. If people gave hugs and kisses to each other, instead of snarfing a box of Twinkies life might be much better.

Exercising regularly is imperative so to encourage this you need to find things you like to do, and a variety of things can encourage you to keep moving instead of falling into terminal boredom. Increasing stamina and losing weight will almost inevitably have a positive effect on your libido. It can reverse some problems with erectile dysfunction in males, and it increases the hormone levels in both sexes that encourage a desire for sexual activity.

Testosterone is the hormone of desire, and both sexes need a certain level of this hormone to be active sexually. It's a good approach to get your levels checked and see where you are because low testosterone can make sex a no-go. In some cases using Viagra or Cialis can help guys who have a bit of trouble getting a good erection and there's no shame in using these things, but these aids should also be addressed with caution because they can have serious side effects for some people.

Some people have crappy sex lives simply because they don't understand the mechanics of what it takes to please their partner. Others are just too lazy to do what it takes to create a dynamic and pleasurable sex life not only for their partners but also for themselves. I've talked to many people in sexless marriages, and when you find a common thread among many that their partner would simply rather masturbate than have sex with them you know, there are serious issues. If they don't find pleasure with their partner and isolate themselves, they are simply blowing off their partner and telling them most plainly that they do not matter.

There are tons of manuals and videos of all types to help with this. No, it's not a porno movie either these are legitimate teaching tools which can help you increase your ability to enjoy sex. If you and your partner explore these together, they can be useful in helping each of your understand the physiology of your partner and also help you learn valuable techniques for giving each other pleasure. The best tool of all though is communication, tell your partner what feels good and guide them to your hot spots. Don't expect them to read your mind this will only leave you disappointed and frustrated. Talk to each other about sex what you like and what you don't like and things that turn you on and off. This should be an ongoing discussion that began before you married and should continue until you end up as dust. The most important thing of all is honesty don't lie about how you feel because you will never like the results.

All that being said one of the most valuable tools you can have in your sexual toolbox is imagination. Having sex the same way at the same time on the same days can get pretty boring pretty fast, and boredom can be a sex killer. To keep your sex life interesting, there are tons of things out there to experiment with. The number of sex toys is astronomical, and there are all sorts of interesting gadgets to play with. There are costumes and all sorts of things that people find interesting but most of all you must bring a willingness to explore each other, and if you have a mutual desire to please each other then you have a better shot at making it for the long haul.

Some people have a hard time with using imagination in sex because they have baggage. Sometimes it's from a bad experience somewhere in the past, or it may be from how they discovered about sex when they were young. It can come from many directions, and it can create challenges to a relationship. But since a relationship is a compromise these things should be brought out and discussed because this is the only possible way that these things can be understood. Loving each other means that you accept warts and bumps of your partner but that doesn't mean that you cannot help them try and find resolution or that ignoring their problems will make them go away. Loving for the long term requires TRUST and since this is the partner you have chosen you really must be open with them, and they must be open to you because trusting each other strengthens your bond immeasurably.

Sometimes, well even often many of us have come to a point where we are being ignored by these people who said they would love honor and cherish us till death do we part. Once that happens, the bond erodes quickly and what was once a relationship turns into something else. It becomes two estranged people in a living arrangement sharing the same space but living separate lives. Many people find this situation intolerable, and divorce soon follows others linger on for years sometimes even until their lives are over often from fear of change or the acceptance that this will be their life.

# Chapter 6.  Red Flags

When we start a new relationship, there is a lot of excitement, and sometimes our judgment can leave a lot to be desired. Many of us have experienced that "what have I done moment" after shall we say a "short-term romance." But there is something far more serious lurking out there that can cause years of misery and more pain and grief for people than almost anything we can imagine. It's called the sexless marriage, and it is the result of a fundamental incompatibility between two people that is so profound that the two people involved might as well be from separate planets and breathing different atmospheres.

There are two distinct types of people involved a first type is an emotional person who places a very high value on intimacy and a sexual connection in their relationship. The second type person does not care about a sexual connection at all and is not interested in intimacy or emotional involvement. You would think that people like this would repel each other like oil and water but for some unknown reason the people that don't care about intimacy seem to want to get a mate that values these things and will often don false colors and pretend that they too value these things in order to get a mate from the first group. Often once they achieve this, they quickly revert to their normal selves and abandon their new mate emotionally.

There are no brands on the foreheads of these pretenders, but from observation, it seems that there are some warning signs (Red Flags) that potentially give them away. Anyone that is interested in an intimate and sexually stimulating marriage should be aware of these things, and if you encounter these things, perhaps you should dig a lot deeper into the potential of your new partner before you make any commitments.

1) Lack of imagination, people that are potentially non-intimate types often lack an imagination and seem to have difficulty creating fantasies. They don't seem to be dreamers or people who think of the future in anything but very concrete terms. They often like to talk about things like houses and possessions and retirement planning and things of this sort are very important to them. They seem to have difficulty with coming up with plans for fun activities and will often leave decisions about what to do up to you. They often don't like choosing which restaurant to go to or picking

31

movies or making decisions about anything such as entertainment or something that is optional. They tend to be very concrete thinkers and will often criticize others for being unrealistic or having their head in the clouds. If you hear this kind of talk and see this kind of behavior beware you are probably looking at a person that will be very closed off and is unlikely to be the type who will be intimate and sexual encounters with this type of person are often only to their satisfaction, they often will make little effort to satisfy their partner. Don't ever think this behavior will get better after you marry them it won't.

2) Has sexual hang-ups: This can indicate a person that has a high degree of sexual inhibitions, and this can lead to disaster. People like this are often at their best immediately before they seal the deal and that will be the best it will ever be, and it will frequently go downhill very fast after that. Many of these people will not participate in oral sex either giving or getting. They also often think of sex as something that is dirty or only for procreation. If you want someone to have a satisfying sex life with this is not the person, and these hang-ups will not go away once you get married. Many people think that after they get married their mate will become more experienced and the sex will improve but in many cases that don't happen. People that have inhibitions and taboos about sharing their body with their mate can cause terrible misery because they will not change. Many people will say it's my body, and I have the right to do what I want with it as an excuse to deny their mate sex but by doing that they had abrogated the vows that they took when they married but they do not care because they believe that their "rights" supersede everything else.

3) Uses religion as an excuse: Some people use religion as an excuse not to have sex with their partner, but this is plainly wrong because the Christian religion advocates sex with a married partner quite plainly and explicitly says that it is wrong to withhold sex from your mate. Many people pretend that they are religious when they are simply being selfish and using religion as a cover.

Religion can also cause some difficulties when people feel that they must be virgins until they are married or that abstinence is their proper form of behavior until marriage. This is a personal belief matter, and if two people agree that this is what they want and believe then it's possible that it may work out, but the difficulty is that it can hide differences in attitude about sex that may later cause horrible difficulties between the couple after they get married. If two people choose to go this route they need to have some very explicit conversations about their sexual beliefs and preferences and they most of all need to be truthful with each other because a mismatch in this area can cause excruciating pain in the relationship and among people that choose not to divorce can lead to a life of misery. Matching someone who expects to have sex twice to three times a week with someone that thinks sex once a month is more than enough will result in unhappiness for at least one partner. This is a place for truth because being in love blinds us to many things and if we choose to ignore these things we do so at our peril.

3) If the sex is bad before you get married it won't get better: A lot of people will marry someone expecting that their sex partner will improve their quality of sex after they get married, that they will become more adventurous in the bedroom and that they will try new things and that the sizzle will amp up after they learn more about each other. This is almost never true. The sex you have before you get married is probably going to be the best sex you will ever have with this person. At that point, their hormones are fully engaged, and they are at their peak of desire for you, and if the sex sucks then, it's likely never going to get any better. If the quality of your sex life is important to you, then you need to do some serious thinking about whether you want to be yoked to this person and whether you are willing to put up with a crappy sex life. Perhaps if you have quantity, maybe you can overlook some of the quality issues, but if you have neither then things start looking pretty bad.

4) A lack of communication about sex: If you have a partner that refuses to talk to you about sex there is a serious problem. This can be a real deal breaker because this is critical to building a good sexual relationship. If you are trying to create an intimate relationship with someone and they won't tell you what feels good or where to touch them or what they like or don't like then you have a serious problem. Someone that is this closed off will never talk about their fantasies and may be the type that doesn't have fantasies, and that is another bad sign. Half of a good sex life is communication telling each other what you like and how to please you and finding out what they need is critical to building the rapport required to make sex interactive. Some people seem to think that their partner should be able to read their mind and just know what they want or need but unfortunately, it doesn't work that way. After we have been together for quite a while, we can sometimes guess, but it's not wise to take it for granted that your partner can figure it out. Communication is critical to any relationship and especially to the sexual part of that relationship, without good communication soon you have two people that end up back to back instead of embracing as lovers.

5) An inability to express emotion: This is a frequent complaint of people engaged in marriage counseling, that one partner will not express emotions they will often walk away or simply ignore their partner if there is

something emotional that they do not wish to deal with (passive-aggressive behavior). Building an intimate relationship with someone that refuses to participate is impossible, and people like this simply refuse to engage in anything that they don't want to deal with. Some will become defensive and even abusive to deflect attention from their inability to deal with emotion intelligently. These people are emotionally immature and don't make good partners because they are more focused on themselves than anything else much like small children they are still only thinking about "Me."

6) We have all laughed at the movies about the 39-year-old mama's boy who has never been on a date who suddenly ends up in a romance. But these people are not good candidates for relationships, few of them are emotionally mature, and their tendency to place their mother or father first over their mate creates havoc it also creates a situation where intimacy is unlikely. This can apply to either sex equally so beware of someone that has never lived on his or her own and is dominated by their parents. These are just some of the things that can show up that are warning signs and unfortunately when we are falling in loving our hormones and the chemistry in our brain can override our good sense and cause us to do some dumb things sometimes. But if you are at least aware of some of the bad things that can happen and you see some of the warning signs maybe a tiny alarm bell will go off in your chemically fogged brain and maybe it will wake up in time to save you from doing something dumb. Or at least wake you up before you tie yourself to the mast of a sinking ship and give you time to run for the lifeboat.

If you've already tried one of these albatross around your neck and have sailed with the Flying Dutchman perhaps, it's not too late for you to regain consciousness and jump over the side and swim to shore.

There are all kinds of reasons that people use to deny their partner intimacy but what it comes down to is that when they married you, they made you promises they are unwilling to keep. Denying your partner an outlet for their sexual needs is abuse, and someone that does this on a regular basis simply doesn't care about how you feel or what your needs might be. They have made a unilateral decision without any consideration for you at all that sex is off the menu. You have been divorced in actuality and have been relegated to the maintenance person.

If this has happened to you, then know this: You Are Not Alone. This has happened to many, many other people as well. If you are the type of person who needs intimate interaction, then it's time to start considering what you might do and how important this is to your future life. We live much longer now than we once did and the prospect of spending decades with someone who has given you the boot stinks. But going it on your own takes some courage, and there are no guarantees. There are tons of websites these days that supposedly match people up, and maybe that's a good thing if they are serious about having some in-depth questionnaires for their participants. But when it comes down to it even living alone can be better than living with someone who does not love you.

Relationships require us to be concerned about each other and sharing our bodies and whatever comes along with each other is what makes marriage tolerable. Being unable to share or unconcerned means you aren't engaged with your partner, and there is no incentive for them to keep putting up with you. Face it relationships are about giving to each other and getting something in return from the relationship. Without that what is the point of this whole exercise in futility?

# Chapter 7. Keys To Making A Relationship Work

Counseling is proving to be a lot less effective than it used to be in resolving sexual problems in relationships (at least judging by the failure rate of marriages and relationships in general). I believe that one of the main reasons for this is that often counselors and therapists are trying to resolve individual problems rather than dealing with the underlying issues. This is, of course, understandable as getting to the heart of a problem can be very difficult, especially as relationships (and expectations of them) have become so much more complex in 21st Century western society. The real answer to any problem is found by going to the source - the root of the problem, rather than just trying to deal with the symptoms. It's the difference between a quick (and difficult) fix and a permanent (and often quite simple) solution.

To illustrate this point, imagine discovering a crack in the wall of your house. To repair it you have two options:

1) Repair the crack. You would buy some plaster and cover over the crack. You might ask for advice on the best way to do this, making sure you have the right tools for the job. You'd then paint or wallpaper over the repaired crack, and it would all look as good as new.
Problem solved - or is it?

The following week a bigger crack appears, and then another. You keep repairing the cracks as they appear - but one day the house falls!

2) Deal with the cause of the crack. Responding this question is going to require some deeper investigation. You're not going to pay too much attention to the crack itself - you'll be checking the foundations, the structure of the house and even the land that the house sits on. You want to find out why the crack has appeared; you're interested in the cause of the problem.

In the process of doing this, you are probably going to discover that the problems with your house are much greater than you thought. It's not really about the wall at all. Some of the grounds of the house may have rotted and need replacing. In the worst case scenario, the land your house is sitting on may have subsidence problems, and the only answer might be to abandon the house entirely and move somewhere else.

Of course, the good news is that once the cause of the problem is eliminated, the problem will disappear for good. It never returns, and you don't have to deal with it on a recurring basis. It may have been more expensive in the first place, but in the long run, it causes you a lot less trouble because it is dealt with permanently. You can get back to enjoying your house for the reasons you decided to move there in the first place - it gives you pleasure as well as shelter and security. It does the job it was designed to do in meeting your life needs.

The above example is remarkably similar to the way our relationships work. If you just 'paper over the cracks' by trying to deal with individual problems, you will never find a happy or lasting solution. And it could simply mean that the result will be a greater disaster later on down the track. Without dealing with the underlying reason of the problem, it will take you a lot more time and effort as the same issues will continue to arise. You might come up with some temporary solutions (which may give you some temporary relief), but the problems will never really go away. However, by putting your attention on the foundations supporting your relationship - and ensuring they are strong - not only will many 'problems' seem just to resolve themselves, but many simply won't arise.

In this book, I deal with the underlying causes for lack of sexual intimacy in a relationship. This isn't about a few ideas on how to perform better in the bedroom. I've broken down the process for getting the sex back into your marriage into five steps. They deal with the causes of the problem rather than the symptoms.

We do this by focusing clearly on the foundations, making sure they are (and remain) strong) and are made of the 'right' materials to support the unique natures of both you and your partner. Do that and not only will the sex come back into your relationship but you will have a level of passion and intimacy that will continue to grow and enrich you both.

## Fixing A Sexless Marriage?

One of the things that continually surfaces in sexless marriages is the desire of one of the partners to fix the sexless marriage. This is almost always the hope of the partner that wants a relationship that has intimacy and sexual connection. But there is an unbeatable problem with this because to fix the problem it requires both partners to recognize that there is a problem and to engage themselves in working to change the conditions in the marriage that cause the lack of intimacy and sexlessness. In most cases, you have one partner that is perfectly satisfied with things the way that they are and has no desire to change things the "refuser" sees no need to change anything and this dooms any hope of fixing things.

One person cannot fix a sexless marriage no matter how hard they try or what exotic means they resort to. Lingerie, scented candles, date nights, and on and on will never change the situation as long as their partner is disengaged from the process. Many people go to extraordinary lengths to change themselves in hopes that this will fix the problem. Losing weight and even having plastic surgery to change their appearance in some cases to try and change how they look. Exercising religiously and dieting have all been tried without any success at all, and none of these things will ever work, and the reason is that they are trying to change another person who has no motivation to change.

Sometimes when it finally comes down to the point where a refused gets ready to walk out the door and delivers an ultimatum, it may appear that there is change, but it is seldom permanent. It is temporary and lasts only long enough to lull the refused back into their accustomed place. The refuser will revert to their previous behavior once things settle down. So lasting change is rare and suspects at best.

In a sexless marriage, hope is often our enemy because it keeps us hanging on far past the point where we should have made the intelligent decision that the relationship will never be what we need and want. At some time you are faced with a choice between staying in a situation where you know you will never have a satisfactory relationship or divorcing and trying to move on and rebuild your life. The divorce rate has risen dramatically as people have chosen to keep trying to find happiness. These days many empty nesters are divorcing after the children are grown so it would appear that many unhappy people stayed married "for the children."

 What effects this has on the children are unclear, but the divorce rate among young people is very high, depending on where you get your statistics it looks as if over half of all new marriages fail within the first eight years. Perhaps some of this is due to the negative influences that these young people experienced growing up in homes where their parents were unhappy. Whatever the cause it is a strong indication that young people are seriously deficient in the skills needed to build good relationships that are successful.

Sex and relationships are probably two of the most important things to humans, but strangely we spend very little time educating young people in the skills necessary to be successful at either of these critical skills. Our approach seems to be a head in the sand kind of way of doing things where we just hope that they will learn it somehow. When I was growing up, we had to figure it out for ourselves because there was no guidance at all because adults never talked about anything remotely connected with sex or relationships. We talked among ourselves and speculated, but real knowledge was scarce.

How we managed to stumble through dating and mating I'll never know and looking back on the results I would say that we really did a pretty poor job of it, and many of us stonewalled our kids just the same way that we were when we were growing up, so I suppose we just passed on the tradition of creating the conditions for misery and divorce along the way. We didn't have the tools to communicate with each other effectively, some learned by trial and error but many never were able to bridge that gap, and many bitter people ended up divorced or even worse staying in a marriage where there was no love. The era of the self-help book brought hope to some; there was a book for everything with a promise that with that book you could fix virtually any problem. Many of the marriage fix it books were no more than directions to buy scented candles and take bubble baths together or schedule "Date Nights" after which everything was supposed to be all fixed only it wasn't. The same problems with the same pain and anger were still there.

If you use Google, you can come up with all kinds of supposed facts and figures one that I keep running across is the claim that there are at least forty million people in the United States living in sexless marriages. That is a huge number, and there is no way that they could ever gather such a number as a fact because for one thing people are embarrassed as hell about being in a sexless marriage, and most would rather be drawn and quartered before they would ever talk about it. But that being said the numbers are still huge and growing, relationships are in trouble, and it seems that there is a division between people that are interested in having intimate sexual type relationships and others that could care less about that and have some other kind of goals in mind.

The problem occurs when you get a person that wants an intimate sexual lifestyle hooked up with the other type. That is a recipe for madness or attempted murder. This is a basic incompatibility, and these types of people should never marry each other, but they do in startling numbers. Because it seems that those other types will camouflage themselves to get a partner. They will pretend to be interested in sex and intimacy and perhaps they are temporarily but long term they have no goals in that direction at all. The problem is that they fool someone that wants an intimate and sexual life into marrying them and after a while, they simply abandon their partner because they think the time for that foolish sexual stuff is over.

This is something that cannot be fixed because in the eyes of the person that has abandoned the sexual and intimate partner there is nothing wrong. They believe that is the way that things should be so there is nothing to be fixed. Of course, they think their partner who wants sex and intimacy is crazy and that they need to be fixed but this is incompatibility at its worst and sadly it sometimes takes years for this drama to play out, and by then there are kids and mortgages and commitments of other types involved. In many cases, this abandonment is a type of abuse of the marriage promises because it was a bait and switch operation where one thing was promised but something else was delivered. To a person that wants an intimate and sexually close relationship, this is a painful and often degrading experience that is destructive to self-esteem and confidence.

So many people get caught up in these sexless marriages, and they are in such pain yet there is little help from counselors. Many don't seem to be equipped to deal with these issues effectively. The self-help gurus offer the scented candles and bubble bath solutions, which are a waste of time and money. Untold millions have been spent on lingerie and sexy outfits to try and lure a partner back into the relationship with no effect. Millions of special dinners and massages and flowers and you name it have all been tried as ways to solve this problem to "Fix" the sexless marriage. But there's nothing really that works because the critical issue is that the refusing partner has to want it to change. Both people have to be fully committed to creating the conditions where both partners can find happiness in the relationship and since this is a pretty good definition of what marriage is about anyway, it seems that once a marriage becomes sexless it ceases to be a marriage, at that point it becomes merely a living arrangement where space and finances are shared.

If you find yourself in a position where you keep trying to fix the relationship, then you need to wake up to the fact that you are trying to do the impossible. One person cannot fix a relationship period it cannot be done. If your relationship has deteriorated so badly that you find yourself living in a sexless marriage without intimacy, then it's time to start facing facts. The recovery rate for sexless marriages is nearly zero, very few people are ever able to turn this around and recreate a working relationship with intimacy and sex again.

At that point you start becoming aware that there are only a few choices that you can make:

1) You can get a divorce and start over and hopefully find a better relationship.
2) You can get your needs met elsewhere either through having an open marriage, an affair or some other arrangement.
3) You can just stay in place and accept things the way they are and learn to live without sex or intimacy.

Each of these choices has pain and difficulties associated with them and the choice is yours to make but to put the choice off just lets the pain pile up and wastes precious time when you could have been living and perhaps enjoying a better life in a new relationship with someone that values you and believes that love, sex, and intimacy are important too. But there are no guarantees that trying to start over will give you a great new life. The older you get, the fewer options there are available. By then the numbers of available prospects has dwindled significantly. Also be aware that many singles in the older group over forty may have been divorced because they were refusers or because they were hard to get along with for some reason. It isn't as easy to find a good partner when you are digging in a dumpster filled with misfits, ex-refusers, and people who have quirks of their own to deal with.

I know that sounds hugely discouraging, but it is possible to get better than what you had if you are cautious enough and keep your wits about you. Unfortunately, many people fall into the same pattern of behavior that got them into trouble in the first place. All of us who have survived a sexless marriage carry scars, and some even have open wounds that will take the time to heal. Many people are also terrified of being alone especially if they lack social skills and a circle of friends to offer some support.

My recommendation at that point is to work on yourself and discover that you can make your happiness. Being happy does not depend on anyone else. It comes from within and recognizing this is a major step forward for many people. Also, consider that once you become satisfied with yourself that you are much more likely to develop healthy relationships with other people and are much more likely to attract a suitable partner.

Life in today's world is challenging, and many people will simply stay in place in their sad world because they lack the courage to strike out on their own. There are valid reasons for staying in place if you can develop a pattern for a living arrangement that works. This is much more common than many people would believe. Some have created long term affairs to satisfy their needs, but this almost always carries a significant danger that it will disrupt the living arrangement because of emotional attachment. Having friends with benefits requires a bit of detachment, and this is beyond many people's ability to manage successfully. We have emotional needs, and we will seek to satisfy those needs somehow whether we sublimate our needs and spend our time and attention on something that distracts us and that can be almost anything, but we often become entangled because we are vulnerable.

# Chapter 8.  Major Issues In Relationships

## Communication

By far this is the most important problem in today's society. True communication does not come with condemnation, and accusations. To truly communicate you have to put yourself out there. That is why I suggest you try communicating just before or after jumping your partner's bones. For some they will only be able to communicate when they are horny as a rabbit. Others will only be able to communicate after an orgasm. Some are not achieving orgasm, and should definitely have a chat with their partner, immediately.

a)  Those that are not achieving orgasm as a couple. Talk with your spouse and explain to them you would like them to watch. Yes, watch you self-masturbate it is super intimate. Often times a partner just needs to see what turns you on! They simply may not have a clue of your desires. And the pure action of watching will be a great communication tool. While in this process you may do it a few times. Each time masturbating invite your partner to take part more and more with your actions. At some point you will find yourself laying in orgasm in his/her hands. I handled her all on my own this round. She just needed to know it was OK. IT IS OK to be vulnerable to your sexual partner. It is ok to lay back, and enjoy the ride 100% at another's will. In all senses at the time of orgasm a person is at their most vulnerable state. With one clear reality "THIS FEELS SO DAMN GOOD!" The thoughts can be anything, but the reality is you must be able to 100% relax, and hand over the reins to another human being, have them help partially or self-masturbate. For intimacy I prefer company!

b)  Those that like communication after orgasm. I suggest, and please take it as pure suggestion. Think hard about what you would like in a sex life. I say this for a reason. Most humans have deep yearning desires/thoughts that are hard to discuss. I take this talk as one of decisive nature. Meaning if you are not having the desires at the time of the talk, well you are a decisive person. Not that this is a horrible thing being decisive, it is a very strong trait. However, if not handled well, this is a dominant feature, it can overwhelm your partner. As well this can be a super strong tool. Allowing you to keep your partner active after sex is a great ability. You might think of tying up your partner and carry on a serious conversation. Actively pursue or discussing your desires after he/she has finished. (With consent of course)....

c) Folks with closet items. They are probably the most common. As they carry huge amounts of yearnings, and fantasy in their mind. They are by far the hardest to get to communicate. Not that A and B do not have secret desires. It is that those who will communicate prior to orgasm more honestly. Well, they have something they want to come out. Meaning they want to try something new that they are inhibited to discuss. This is 90% of society. I do not have any exacting polls. I do have vast experience in this area though. Most humans have a large problem expressing, and living their fantasy. Not just in the bedroom, but in their everyday life. They work there 9-5, pay bills and hide their secrets. No more, it is time to bring these fantasies/desires out with your life partner! We have become content settling for the way things are, instead of creating a life we desire.

## Inhibitions

A percentage of society has had their best orgasm climbing a pole! Hmm who would have guessed that one? Bondage, a huge percentage of the population has bondage desires. Some to a large degree, others to a small degree, and this is an inner desire to submit, and turn over control. No reason to be inhibited. Your spouse is your best friend, and they will work with you through these desires. As long as they know what is truly on your mind! If they do not know, and you have not expressed your desires then you will just be frustrated. Often times going to bed frustrated, mad or angry is from lack of communication, sexual activity or not feeling good about you. When reading this book put these practices to work. You will achieve better sleep at night!

## Secret Desires

These are the last to come out. I used to have a secret desire to tie up my wife and have my way with her. It turned out, my true desire was to have her tie me up, and have her way with me. Funny thing telling your spouses will really open up your true desires. Often times while enacting your desires you will find out you wanted the opposite. It is great to know the truth!

## Embarrassment

Nothing to be embarrassed about! Absolutely nothing! How do I stress this, there is absolutely nothing to be embarrassed about! You are human, and sexual feelings and desires occur daily. It is not as though you have any control over them! Your mind is amazing, and it will self-populate anything from Forced Bisexual experience to being whipped to being just loved. From having your spouse's bend you over, and doing you anal to any other list of items. There is nothing to be embarrassed about! Your mind will populate fantasies, and desires throughout life.

## Anger And Unresolved Issues

90% of the time they come from not acting or communicating your desires. You will not know your true desires till you communicate them. Once that is done you will find your true desires coming out by the boatloads. If you repress all your thoughts, and desires you will be angry, frustrated, and overall depressed throughout parts of your life. After communication i will warn you! You can now be angered by putting yourself out there. Do not ask your spouse to do this then not act on some of the fantasies they have! Really how dare you expose your spouse's deepest yearnings, and leave them lying on the floor! If I was there, I would leave you on the floor, and take your spouse, on a fantasy tour. If you do not think someone will, well just wait on the divorce papers. People will only live so long angry in a marriage before realizing it is just as easy, to be mad, and alone. If you do not think a lot of our high divorce rate is for sexual inadequate partners, and sexual none active partners you are miss informed. Read my Top Ten reasons for divorce by David Xzenre.

## Time

Such a simple thing there is even a song for it "Take time to make time to be there!" JUST MAKE THE Fricking Time to give your spouse orgasms, and feeling of appreciation! You take time to make time to be there, period no exceptions! If not interested in that statement; just close the book, and go back to your angry repressed world. You take time to figure some unique method of giving your spouse a orgasm. Then you make time to do this activity! When the thought is laid out put steps in motion to achieve the new goal!

## Goose And Gander

If you are not satisfying your spouse 100%! Why would they take time to satisfy you? No room for wiggles here. The only wiggling will be your spouse, and you in bed if you follow some of these simple things. I do say simple because they are simple and fun! At first they will seem Greek. Then they will be first nature! Notice not second nature. First natural order of things is of an adult male and adult female to procreate. Second society stereotype is to become discontent prudes! I prefer to keep first nature alive and well.

It is safe to say that a huge percentage of males who have fantasies of anal. They have fantasies of being done anally. Nothing wrong with that the male G spot is in an inconvenient location, wives. They are not gay! They just want to know what it's like and to feel the strength of a wife to take them. They want to be the one squirming all over the bed.

Has your spouse always wanted a threesome? You can put a halt to it in seconds or create a hell of a time. WIFE: "Ok, honey I will do a threesome. First, find a guy to do it with first. I want to see you do the guy and help him, do you? I will help him! I also want both you guys to do me at the same time." Hmm probably not the threesome your husband had in his conscious mind. Careful though it is the fact that over half the men, in the world although not gay, have a secret of being screwed by another man. He might say yes to this.... If he does, again it does not make him gay. A few sexual activities or encounters between two men or two ladies do not make them gay. A gay person simply prefers one sex, the same sex as themselves. They have no desire to be with the opposite sex often starting from the early years. A person who experiments? Well, that is all it is, experimenting, and testing their inner desires, and testing limits. I hardly think of such a person as BI Sexual. I think about bisexual as an ongoing passage. Right from late teens through adulthood enjoying both sexes. Having sex with both males and females over a period of years. That is a bisexual. If you ever do threesomes have strict rules. "NO KISSING/CUDDLING THE THIRD PERSON! And PROTECTION!" Goose and gander wow it goes so far. Anything you have done or want to do with your spouse, they can now do to you! Your wife wants a sensual spanking? Well, maybe the wife should give you a corporal spanking. Your spouse wants to be tied up? They could demonstrate what they want on you! Goose and Gander what a wonderful thing. Not only can you achieve some of your fantasies, but you can experience your spouse's fantasies.

## The List

This item is so important for communication. Often when communicating, we cannot honestly say what we are thinking. We might start to say it but cannot put it out there. Write a list of what you would like, your secret desires, your cravings. Have it at hand when talking with your spouse. You may also, just hand it to them, and discuss it after they absorb it. Heck makes a copy, and go thru the list one item at a time with your spouse. If you both have your list in the open, it is a GREAT THING! Now you know your spouse's inner most desires! I am not saying everything on a list is mandatory. I am saying explore your partner's desires. Share verbally, and physically the ones you can achieve. Discuss the ones you are not comfortable at this time achieving. I warn you both if it is on the list there is a reason. Some desires/fantasies are very strong and a top reason for infidelity. If your spouse has a super strong desire they are already mentally seeking a person to enact them with.


## BDSM

I am no BDSM expert. If this is on your list, you will have to do your homework. I know light bondage only. Tying spouse to the bed or from a ceiling hook. I guess some punishment for I have received light whips, belts, canes, etc.. while in this position with a spouse/girlfriend. The full defines of BDSM are much larger though, and best explained by someone in the full lifestyle. Nothing wrong with it, I just do not have vast experience in the subject matter.

## Doing Things You Do Not Like?

I do many things in life I do not like. Work for a boss I hate. Deal with idiots in the world that piss me off. Why on earth would not I do a few things or a lot of things for my spouse? In fact, it might have just been a subconscious lie me not liking something. I might do them and say "WOW, why did I think I would not like that?" Sometimes I really will not like it. But, if it makes my spouse happy and achieves orgasm or happiness I am in. Then what's the harm in me doing things I do not like? No harm at all, give your spouse the things they want in the bedroom they will return the favor. As I said, humans are by nature giving souls!

 If your spouse loves you, and is part of the family unit. I would think hard about what I "WILL NOT DO". There is nothing I will not do for my spouse! Absolutely nothing! There are things I do not like, that is just part of life!

## Your Spouse Has No Desires?

Bullshit! But ok, I will play along. If your spouse has no secret desires or sexual urges great! It is like these blank sheets of paper in front of me. I get to discover every taboo my spouse has. I do mean every taboo! Your spouse has just written a blank check, hope they can cash it! If you give your spouse a blank sheet of paper? Hmm well that means they can just try anything to see if it is in your invisible fantasy list.

## The Evolving Mind

 Last week you liked being on the bottom. This week your mind changed your position to being on top. Point being, your mind will continue to wander, and change its logic. If logic applies to anything about orgasm it is changing and doing new things. Your mind will change, and you must have open discussion ability with your mate. Yep, back to drawing board for discussion, and letting your spouse in your mind. These are not always deep dwelling discussions. Just simply by the way honey "I think I want to" Or not say a word and just take it. As well a quick web link of what you are thinking or a quick email to your spouse.

### Non Sexual Gratification

Wow wives complain about this one! Clean garage, I want a green yard, I want trees, I want cleaner home. Husbands or Dominate partner Please open your eyes look around. What can you do this week to make your spouse's life more pleasant in a no sexual manner! It could be as easy as planting a tree or throwing junk out around house, removing clutter. Wives and now dominate partners take notice of phrase throw junk out. No need to clutter a home with items you have not touched in 90 days. In fact if you have an item you have not touched in 90 days. I challenge you to go throw it away! Remove clutter it will create a clear mindset. It will also enable you to not buy more clutter thus allowing you to save more cash to make your income winner's life easier!

When is the last time you gave your spouse a thorough back rub? Do I need say anymore? Ok, maybe so, is your spouse in the kitchen going give them a backrub! Plenty of oils in a kitchen.

### Physically Fit

If you are out of shape well get your ass up, and put away the Bon Bon's, and work out. Take a walk on the beach. Walk down the block, do sit-ups, do push-ups do something! Do Something! The vast number of discontent people is only outweighed by the pure lazy overweight folks. Get up, and be active, grab life by the horns so you can LIVE IT! You want a more sexually active life? Then get in shape, and be more sexually desirable/able.

### Sex Therapy?

If you go to a sex therapy and complain that your spouse wants to do some obscure thing. The therapist most likely in the back of their mind is thinking. "Man would I like to get this person tied up, and straightened them out. They need a good old fashion kinky fuck. Better yet maybe a spanking will help break them down!". Your spouse is your sex therapist do not be silly, go to them and talk. Go to them, and have sex! Go to them, and give them an orgasm now! Everything will work itself out if sexually satisfied. Go to them and tell explain a fantasy. Do something!

### Health Problems?

Really this is the one item that is not fixable. If your spouse is laid up with a heart attack, cancer, death bed? There is not much this book can help on.

Although if I was on my deathbed; I would prefer to die right after a good old orgasm.

### *Give Your Spouse An Orgasm!*

If I need to say to do it spontaneously? You have not been reading and should start at page 1 again. I have listed just a few things below you can do spontaneously.

# Chapter 9.  The Dance Of The Sexless Marriage

We have seen how difficult it is for men is to connect emotionally, not only through sex.  We have seen why they are pulled towards and strongly away from the women they love.  We know that both partners end up starved of satisfying the basic human need for sex.  We have seen why even waging conflict doesn't resolve the issue.  What, then, if any, is the reason to be in and continue  within a sexless marriage?

Both sides are trapped in what we can call the Dance of the Sexless Marriage:

I withdraw, not to be hurt by him;
BUT he is hurt by my withdrawal;
so he dumps me before I dump him

Distressed couples get caught up in a negative dance, where each reacts to the other by the expected behaviors dictated by their attachment model than from real perceptions, both sides perpetuating the negative spiral of rejection and abandonment this way. Sue Johnson's helps couples dissect their debates and dig deeper beyond the usual fights about dirty dishes and financial spats. That is because a couple's  repetitive arguments are really about either one or both partners "not feeling securely attached."

This is a couple where there is not a person with a secure attachment, and where both are deeply insecure of being worthy of being loved by the other.....Each partner describes their "steps in the dance:" "The more I (here the main behavior of one partner)_, the more you (here the repetitive response of the other partner)_."

Alisha gets upset every time her husband invites his friends over to watch football every Sunday afternoon without first discussing it with her.  She tries to get his attention a couple of times and then finally explodes Sunday nights. "You always have your friends over on Sundays. You want food and drinks and take over the living room. You never give me notice or ask if I mind. When I try to talk to you about something while they are here, you just walk away and go back to them and the game!  The more I try to tell you I am frustrated, the more you get upset with me and tell me I never "let you have guy time!"  Why don't you think about me at all? It's like you don't even care!"

Darren responds with exasperation, "You always bring your issues up while the guys are here. You know I can't talk then and am trying to relax and have a good time. I don't see why you get upset about it. I need to spend time with my friends, and you should know they're coming by now, that's what we always do. Why can't you let me do my thing? The more you nag me about something so little, the more I want to get away from the same old argument, I don't even want to deal with it anymore."

Doing this kind of interaction creates two irreducible positions, and both are unable to listen to the needs of the other's demands...
Being able to step out of the cycle of reciprocal accusations allows both insecurely attached partners to observe the repetitive nature of their interaction.

They see the cycle of defense against rejection that works as real perceived rejection by the other, who needs to act more rejecting to preserve his self. In this way, they can see their behaviors as asking for and rejecting intimacy at the same time....

Let's now apply this dance to the sexual arena and see how it works: sing sex as a tool for control;
"My boyfriend is often sarcastic, putting me down... like if I forget to do something, he'll sneer, "Nice job!" Or if I don't hear something he said or mishear him he will fly off the handle and call me a horrible listener. The worst is when I'm not in the mood for sex (surprise), and then he'll make snide comments and refuse to speak to me, sometimes for days. Usually, I end up sleeping with him because I want to feel close again and I can't stand being ignored for so long. The sex is excellent when we have it, but I don't feel safe, and am bothered by his inability to climax from regular sex since he gets angry when I don't "finish him off." On the other hand, I climax easily, but I wouldn't be angry if I didn't.

So, all this means that sex, which should be fun, is stressful since I know I'll be in trouble if I don't do things for 40 minutes after I finish that I sometimes find physically uncomfortable or painful. He tells me I'm completely selfish and as his partner should satisfy him after I get off. I feel guilty, and I want closeness.

When I try to speak about my feelings about the relationship, or even things going on in my life unrelated to him, he shuts me down, either because what I'm saying is boring or because he's not in the mood to talk. "Why should he give me communication, what I want, when I don't give him sex, what he wants?" he points out over and over

51

If both parties could see the interaction from this point of view: "The more I behave in a fearful way towards sex with you, the more you demand my collaboration and force me to do things I'm not happy with." The more I fear that you are not connected with me, the more I push you to do things for me that I want but repel you."

As is clear here, both are pushing each other to be more anxious and avoidant, using sex as a tool for control and blocking the emotional connection between them....

The solution is to stop; recognize the actions that make the other more fearful of abandonment or control, and ask: what would be the way to have you more comfortable with the relationship? What can we do to give each other the feeling of being understood in the basic fears and being also respected in the expressed needs?

## Using Sex As A Tool For Punishment

"It seems so weird saying this, but I have to beg my husband for sex. It didn't use to be this way. It seemed a little strange to me that after we made love, I wouldn't hear from him for the next day or two, but when I asked him, he brushed it off like it wasn't a big deal, he was happy with how things were, and we were both adults, we didn't need to talk every single day. I trusted him, so I tried to be okay with it and just figured out as our relationship grew, we'd spend more time together. Our relationship did grow, but the more time we spent together, the less we had sex. Now we are married, and it's almost never.

It's not like we fight all the time or anything. Sometimes we may even have a great day together, then we get home and start kissing, and suddenly he shuts down and pulls away and makes up an excuse about having to be up early or something. Everybody says men always want sex, so I don't know what to think! Does he not think I'm pretty anymore? Is he cheating on me? If he doesn't want me, why is sweet to me at all? I feel so ashamed, a woman who has to beg for sex from a man??? I am so embarrassed I don't even want to tell anyone."

Here is the raw deal that a sexless marriage proposes: he can be together with her, share daily time and projects, but shut her out of any intimacy. As long as she takes this distancing as part of her deal, he will not be confronted with his resistance to intimacy. This is the fault line in this marriage: he is not fulfilling his part of the love contract in a marriage: "We will take care of each other's needs for love and connection." Knowing what we know about attachment, is possible now to think of a path to change this situation.

52

First, she needs to own her frustration. If she continues without confronting the situation, this will continue deteriorating and get to nowhere fast. He will not love her more if she continues to be silent and giving him the perception that nothing happens when he refuses sex. She denies her own needs, why should he attend to them?

Let's suppose that she had a somehow secure attachment, loves herself and is very focused on what makes her happy. She is in touch with what bothers her, no denial or excuses here.
If she is secure, she will feel worthy of love and attention, so she can ask for what she needs without anger. If she has an insecure attachment, perhaps she will keep silent up to the moment when she fills with negative feelings and explodes with recriminations or critical comments. What happens with this kind of communication, is that it confirms to the avoidant partner that he needs to withdraw more to avoid accusations! The only solution for the anxious partner willing to get a positive response is to practice self-centering (or use meditation) and immediately express herself. Nothing gained using the pursue-withdrawal dance here.

Here are the steps:

1) Begin describing the situation in the panoramic view proposed before:
The more you avoid us being affectionate with each other, the more I feel frustrated without reason."
The more I feel frustrated and emotionally starved, the more you withdraw from intimacy."

2) "Let's agree that this situation is unhealthy and will end up destroying our marriage. We married with the assumption that this was also a sexual contract because both have needs for love and connection. Now, having a sexless marriage is not part of the agreement."

3) "I want to try to be a secure contact with you. I watch my promises, so you can be sure that I deliver to you what I promise, so there are no disappointments in my behavior. I want you to acknowledge that I'm consistent with you and that you share what feelings you have when you see that I'm here for you."

4) "You need to know that I'm sure about my sexual needs. They are a piece of who I am and the happiness I deserve in a relationship. In short, sex is non-negotiable for me."

"When you don't follow up with more intimacy when we are together, I feel that I'm on thin ice. Can you tell me what the sexual frequency that you feel good about is?"

5) Show real concern for him and his needs satisfaction: "I hope that you can tell me exactly what is that you need to feel better about intimacy so that we can face this challenge together."

In short: the partner who feels in control of the situation because has a more secure attachment, and can function as a secure base for the other, have to keep alive the conversation about reciprocal sexual needs.

# Chapter 10.  Building a Secure Adult Attachment

Does it matter if your partner's feelings are equally as strong as yours? Probably to a certain degree… for women it is a given that they are willing to take risks associated with being vulnerable on many levels, for them, this is the ideal form of connection with a loved one, and the only one that nurtures her connection needs.  But you know that men and women are experiencing intimacy differently, and it cannot be compared exactly. Sometimes you may wonder how to test the other person's level of needed intimacy; to be unsure if you both desire and need the same closeness is damaging. Now you know that fights, disputes, and heated arguments sometimes cover up a hidden question: "Do you care about this as much as I do?"

Again, when you need trust and intimacy, it is worth it to explore carefully, respectfully but deeply, what are the reciprocal needs for intimacy…any person who experiences your needs as too demanding, and plans to hold back, will be a constant source of frustration and loneliness. It is important that the person near you values and needs a degree of intimacy similar to yours. Now, you know what to look for!  When you do find this person, the real game of being near begins!

## Securely Attached

In a secure relationship, both partners can pay attention to their behaviors and identify the feelings and needs associated with and causing them. They notice any change in their closeness and connection and can communicate effectively about what they are experiencing and needing.

The rift would widen between them as each partner's needs go unspoken and unmet, and the hurt produced by the failure of the other to know and solve your needs is the worst feeling you can have.

### Create A Secure Attachment

As you have learned, it is important to determine not only your attachment style but that of your partner, especially if you experiencing extensive conflicts in your relationship over intimacy.  You may be wondering if there is a test to simplify this process - there is!  Take this test to identify your attachment style. If your partner is willing to take the test honestly as well, great. Otherwise, you can use your new knowledge to get a good idea of what attachment style he is dealing with the world through.

Think about these aspects of your partner:

• Do you know about his childhood and his relationship with his primary caregiver?
• What about some of his romantic relationships in the past?
• What are his current friendships like (Does he have any? Are they close? Does he trust them and talk openly with them?)
• What are some of the things he says about relationships or other people? (e.g.,. "You can't trust anyone. I've always been independent; it's easier/better that way.")
• Does he describe you or others as needy or dependent in a negative way?
• Does he seek out intimacy with you and accept intimate gestures from you without reprisal or backpedaling?
• If he is closed off to you or others and grew up with cold or indifferent family ties, he is probably working on an avoidant attachment style.
• If he pulls away from you sometimes, but tries to connect with others, or seems to want more, but "gets scared" he likely has an insecure attachment style.
• If he is comfortable getting close to you, his friends, and sure of himself and his "place in the world" he has a secure attachment style.

### Spouse As Evil Villain

Up until now, you believed that the isolation and the withholding of sex, etc. that your husband is doing is because he is bad, but it is because he doesn't know any better. It doesn't matter who you are; this is the only way he has of connecting with you. It's a lousy way, it is pitiful, but he is trying to connect.

If you can keep this in mind, it will help you to decrease some of your anger, therefore guards against, your husband. See him as a refugee from a childhood upbringing that left him scarred and unable of connecting at a deeper level, but still wanting to, as we all do. It is not a reflection of your sexiness or worth as a female. It is simply that the two of you are operating out of different models of the world with different methods of creating and maintaining relationships.

Knowing this about yourself and your partner, are you a good match for your intimacy needs?

If you come to the resolution that you are mismatched on attachment styles, probably you can have a big feeling of relief now....it makes sense! Endless discussions that led nowhere happened because you both were seeing the world through different lenses!

Viewing the world in completely different ways makes it difficult to come to an understanding on anything, especially without knowing that is what is causing the problem to begin with. Now you know that it probably answers a lot of questions you have had about why your relationship "just doesn't seem to work."

Nobody is "bad" but people are mismatched because of ignorance, youthful confusion and other reasons. After so many years of needs for love and connection being frustrated, perhaps behaviors are seen as hurtful and cruel, just because they keep hitting on the same wounds of needs chronic frustration.

### *Mourning The Spouse You Needed*

You may now be at the point where you realize that the "perfect man" you married, your "ideal mate" is not so ideal or perfect for you after all. This union doesn't complete you because he also lacks a secure attachment; and he can't give you what he also is lacking. This is a difficult realization, though it is an important one. It is a realization that will get you "unstuck" from the negative cycles you have been living in and allowed you to move forward.

For example, you might be stuck on the idea of demanding from him what you think he refuses because of nastiness, -a loving connection- because you are fighting him to maintain the illusion of the one man you thought you married...Kind of: "if I insist on him being loving to me, I will get him to be loving; it's only a question of making him know how I feel...and he will change!" Now, you give up this last illusion: he can't be loving because his avoidant attachment never taught him how to provide and receive love.

With this realization comes a deep sense of loss. The man you thought you found, married, and would be with for the rest of your life is, in a sense, gone. Some of the pain you have probably even identified to yourself at times throughout your marital challenges is that you "miss the man [you] fell in love with/married." Missing someone is always difficult.

It's okay to miss that man, and to miss the happiness you had early on that was based on "finding and loving him" to begin with. You got confused and swept away by some of the misconceptions about love and marriage society fed you, and there was never a serious talk about the kind of partner you needed.

Now that you understand that you always needed a secure attachment in marriage, and discover that you got one with an avoidant person with whom you cannot even talk about building a secure bond....there is a sense of loss.

This is the right time for mourning that loss. Feel it, accept it, allow yourself to be sad over letting go of that misconceived "him" or "her." Mourning your loss will give you the release you need to take that first step towards change and happiness, however bad or difficult that may feel right now.

### *Decide To Stay Or To Leave*

Paying attention to your needs, and accepting them as legit and valid, and observing the marriage you are in now, shows that there is a gap between what you need and what you have. Accepting both of those facts as true is a starting point of both your grieving and you moving forward.

The next step in your life is to make the difficult decision of whether to stay in this "new" marriage to a man you need to get to know all over again and learn to manage the mismatch in your needs for intimacy, or leave the marriage to find someone with whom your attachment styles would be better matched.

This is, obviously, not a decision lightly made and only you can make it. Perhaps you need to make lists of pros and cons of the actual situation. Enlist help, from a counselor or trusted friends, as to have a balance of opinion to help you decide better.

Some things to consider that may assist you, depending on your priorities and beliefs are:

1) How old are you? How many years have you been married?
2) Do you have children? Ages? Their degree of independence from you?
3) How frustrated your needs for love and connection are?
4) Do you see yourself having legitimate expectations to be loved?
5) Do you still love the man he is, not just the man you thought he would be?
6) How do you see your husband now that you know more about why he does what he does/his attachment style?
7) Are you still angry with him, despite the new understanding offered here?

8) Knowing he cannot change, or do better, by himself, are you willing to help him and struggle with new challenges until things improve?

9) Will you be able to feel good within your relationship with your new knowledge about attachment styles, your needs, and your husband's behavior?

10) Do you feel like it would be better to start over, or to work with what you have now?

## Staying And Creating A Secure Attachment

If you are married to an avoidant spouse, they will obviously be not only uncomfortable but down right resistant to talking about the issues outlined in this book. However, their attachment style is creating passive aggressive behaviors and damaging your relationship and must be recognized by them, as well. If they do not recognize and take ownership of their behaviors and their consequences, there is little you can do to help them change the behaviors and the relationship.

By nature, your partner knows there are relationship problems, and that they are causing many of them, consciously or subconsciously. Let them know that you are aware there are issues, that you love them and are willing to take responsibility for your part of the problems, but that you also need them to do the same so that things can get back on track. If you simply attack and blame them, the cycle will merely continue, despite anything you could learn about passive aggression and attachment. Instead, tell them what you have learned about attachment styles: yours and theirs, as somehow mismatched and how they affect your relationship and that you think it would help both of you if they learn too. They can do this learning in several ways:

Once they recognize and accept how their attachment style is preventing them from meeting their needs and yours and their resulting behavior and consequences, you can begin working together to make changes in your relationship. Building a secure attachment takes work and time, you need some suggestions to get started.

## Be Each Other's Champion

First, if you haven't already, make a list of Needs Satisfaction within your marriage. During a time when the two of you are calm, let your spouse know that you are concerned about their needs and would like for them to make the same list you did so that you can be a better partner. Share that you want to talk about the lists together when they are finished. Having made the lists, you get a better idea of the areas missing.

Next sit down together to talk about your lists. Make this a low-stress occasion, sit where you are both comfortable, make tea or turn on some music for example.

You can both print out your lists and therefore have a map for the discussion. You will each have a better understanding of what each feels is missing to repair the damage caused by an insecure attachment and a clear, effective and "safe" way to communicate the concerns to one another.

Try to stay focused on the results of the lists, giving specific examples, but not straying to other problems or dumping blame on each other.

Cover each issue, question and answer from both partners before moving on to the next so you can see the discrepancy or area for improvement.

Trade and keep your lists, so you have a reminder of what your partner needs from you.

Make a plan with clear and simple, achievable goals for each of you to do something for your partner based on the needs list in the next week.

Each week come together again and talk about the results of your efforts. Acknowledge the effort your partner made, tell him how good it feels to have him cooperating with you, and make new goals, this time either make two separate efforts or shorten the deadline to 3 days. Soon you will be thinking of your partner's needs and vice versa and will be able to both make and acknowledge efforts to meet one another needs.

Once you become more attuned to your partner's needs, and he to yours, go the extra step and check in with him when you notice one of his needs being neglected, ignored or set aside for whatever reason, even if it is not due to anything to do with you. Tell him you noticed and asked what you can do to help correct the situation. (eg. You notice he is having to spend more time at work this week and are concerned about him missing his Tuesday poker night with his friends which he said is important to him. Maybe you could pick up beer and pizza and drop it off at his office so he can go straight there after work.)

Don't forget to pay attention to his sexual needs, especially if you are starting to feel more comfortable and therefore not "needing" the physical affection as desperately as before when you needed it as confirmation of being loved. If he is acting in the sweet ways you want him according to what makes you feel like being intimate with him, then remember to be intimate with him! Try initiating, even if it is unusual for you. Sometimes, some simple kissing on the neck can get him started, and he will take over getting you excited. If your attempts are rejected, remember, it is not because you are unattractive, there is something unrelated going on! Don't blow up, and don't let this punish you by diminishing your confidence.

Also, we know men need sex for different reasons than women. Is that work situation making him stressed and tired? Maybe you could give him release in a way he needs one night - quick, simple, etc., without requiring the time and attention you usually prefer. You may find you enjoy the closeness despite what you imagined. If you just don't feel you can be that simplistic about it, do something to make yourself feel sexy before or after, take a bath, put on your favorite smell-good lotion, read an erotic story, etc.

There is a lot of work to do, but some of it can be not only productive but comforting and pleasant. And none of it has to be done all alone. Don't forget, you are not the only person to go through this, and there is a considerable help in the area of attachment and relationship healing.

Rebecca had been struggling in her marriage for years, but still loved Darryl and decided to stay and work through this with him.
"I was feeling empowered by learning about what was happening in my marriage, but I was still scared of addressing all these issues with him. After all, the whole point was that we hadn't been connecting or understanding each other for a long time, maybe ever really.

This wasn't something ever taught in school or talked about by mothers and aunts, but I realized that didn't mean it was never experienced or talked about by anyone. So I looked for a therapist who would understand about different attachment styles. I found someone who was willing to work not only with me but with Darryl when he was ready to join us or even talk on his own. This gave me a place to talk safely and someone from whom I could gain real insight. To my surprise, Darryl joined us pretty soon after I told him I was concerned for his needs and as well as for us as a couple. It was great having an atmosphere of safety, support and unbiased conversation in which we could talk about our hidden needs. It helped us be respectful towards each other and to unveil some of these things we had worked so hard, but so unconsciously, at hiding all these years. No need to hide now, knowing what our styles make us do to each other...he is not my enemy, and he laughs now at the memory of defending himself from me by avoiding sex. I have also gotten a little more comfortable talking with friends I trust about my relationship and have found some great books and resources to learn more about the challenges we are facing. We fall back sometimes, but in general, we are communicating so much better, and I can feel it changed so many things in my life."

# Chapter 11.  Taking Things For Granted

One thing that happens to many relationships is that people start taking each other for granted with an expectation that the other person will stay around no matter what you do them. This is a short road to destruction of the love and trust that are needed to keep a relationship alive.

Human beings have a need for attention from others, and normally there is also a craving for touch. Touching each other helps reaffirm the bond that makes a relationship work, and when a marriage goes sexless, the bond begins to erode. Without the loving touch from our partner, we are essentially living alone in a hostile environment.

Being unwilling to share your body with your partner is a rejection of huge magnitude because it tells them plainly that you don't care if they have needs and that you have withdrawn from the partnership. This is painful and creates resentment that may not be consciously recognized immediately, but eventually, it usually becomes clear that the relationship that existed when the relationship began is over.

A lot of refusers don't see anything wrong with this abandonment, and they will often just tell you to suck it up buttercup this is the way it is. They rely heavily on your lack of resolving to keep you in place. If you start to become rebellious and start making changes, they will often put on a mask and attempt to lure you back into your chains of solitude. But the mask is only pretended and as soon as they feel that you have been roped back in their previous behaviors usually return.

Nobody is a perfect partner and the levels of interaction in a relationship almost always have ebb and flow that changes over time. But the real and only thing that makes a real solid relationship is a commitment by both partners to creating some happiness for both parties. No one is going to be happy all the time, and without a doubt, there will be serious trials placed on a relationship of any duration, but as long as there is a whole hearted commitment to keeping the relationship alive, it can thrive. Loving is not for the faint of heart or for those who just seek casual gratification it is a serious business because it requires that two people stay engaged with each other often under trying circumstances.

There will be anger and hurt at times but if both partners can keep focused on the idea that they still love each other more than half the battle is already won. Human beings are not monogamous by nature this is a learned behavior, and it requires using our big brain for more than holding up the top of our heads. When we first fall in love, we are supercharged with a hormone soup that leaves precious little brain power for rational thought. We can become obsessed with our new love and spend tons of hours daydreaming and scheming to get what we want from them. At that point, that hormone soup is screaming for sex because that is the most intimate thing that two people can do. To share your body with your lover releases yet another flood of hormones which is nature's way of keeping the human race supplied with new people.

At this point, even bad sex can be perceived as good because those hormones distort our emotions. This opens us to a huge danger because we have created an image in our mind of what our love is like and when seen through this chemical haze we often make long term decisions based upon this false image that we have created. A great many people have married someone only to discover that almost everything they hoped and dreamed the other person would be is a self-made myth. Reality can be sobering, and sadly a great many relationships do not survive the big reveal. Many times once the hormones begin to calm down the face palm gesture and the thought "What have I done" shows itself as the reality begins to sink in. There are several possible outcomes at this point. Many people hit the parachute and bail out that's why the divorce rate among newly married people hits around 53% by the seventh year of marriage. This is a huge number and a big indicator that we suck at relationships. But there are also other outcomes possible if two people are flexible enough and committed to each other and LOVE each other with more than just a passing physical lust they can build their place that they share and where there is some happiness for both parties. But that takes work, and many people just don't want to make that effort, and the major reason behind all their excuses is that they are selfish. They simply don't care enough about the other person or the relationship to give of themselves.

Selfishness is, in my opinion, the number one relationship murderer; people who cannot get outside themselves enough to care for their mate are rejecting the other party most emphatically. Withdrawing from the touch and interaction of sex in the relationship is throwing down the gauntlet and saying you are not important enough to me that I will do things just for the sake of your happiness. This happens often, and usually over a period but in the end, it is a destroyer of trust, and that trust is necessary for any relationship to survive.

In many cases the relationship becomes distorted, and you have one person who gives a lot and the other who just takes a lot. When you have this kind of imbalance eventually the giver will get used up until they no longer have any desire to keep giving. The taker may be demanding and critical which is certainly not a loving characteristic. This outlook certainly emphasizes the negative things that can happen when you have a twisted relationship that lacks balance as well as equality between the partners.

What can be done about all this you might ask? Well, we have this thing between our ears that is holding up the top of our heads, and it can be quite useful if it is sensibly applied. The first determining factor is a commitment by both parties involved. This has to be an all in all cards on the table commitment to sharing everything good, bad and indifferent. This implies that both people will work together and to do that effectively it requires the Loving Touch. This is a term that I use to describe intimacy which is the place where trust is born between two people. A good relationship is a touching relationship not always sexual but always genuine. This is the most positive way to communicate on a level that strengthens the bond between two people. In effect, you are saying I trust you with everything that is me when you share your bodies with each other. This does two very important things it lets your partner feel that you are concerned for their happiness when you give them pleasure, and it also reboots some of those endorphins that you initially felt when you began the relationship.

This is the time to leave your hang-ups outside the bedroom door everyone has their little pleasures that they enjoy and being willing to give each other those things is a huge expression of both trusts and caring. The Kama Sutra (No not the dirty movie you heard about in High School) outlines almost all the possibilities for a male and female to interact physically with each other. Most people have two or three ways that they perform sex at most. This can lead to boredom with the sex act and sometimes causes couples to get stale and quit being interested at all. It takes will and imagination for two people that have been together for a long time to keep things interesting. This requires conscious thought and planning. (I can hear you moaning now about how sex is supposed to be spontaneous). Whoever put that into your head was full of shit, if you have been married a while and have kids, you know without fail that spontaneous sex is almost nonexistent it takes a master planner to steal enough time to make the beast with two backs.

Great planning makes great sex because it allows you to use your imagination. Your brain is your largest sex organ, and the trigger for orgasm lives there. There are people who can think themselves into having an orgasm without any other stimulus that tells you something incredibly important. That being that the largest part of sex is mental. Physical stimulation triggers the mental setup that creates the orgasm. What I mean to point out here is that sex doesn't necessarily always involve the external sex organs as the primary erogenous zone. Our whole bodies are sex organs that are capable of being stimulated in a multitude of ways that we find pleasurable. Getting to know your partner's trigger points is what love is all about, and it's about the most fun two people can have PERIOD. That is why it is so incredibly painful to be rejected by your partner when they deny you the sharing of the sexual experience. A good relationship requires an extraordinary amount of closeness and the ultimate expression that we are capable of to reinforce that closeness is getting the skin on skin with our partner wearing nothing but a smile. One thing that many refusers often say is "It's just sex" as if that were a minor thing, but it isn't minor at all it is the glue that holds a relationship together.

Some people as they age can no longer participate as they did when they were younger but does that mean they cannot enjoy a sexual experience? Not at all, it merely means that it's time to get inventive and bring that imagination to the game once again. There are huge numbers of ways to stimulate someone sexually without having traditional intercourse, but the proof of the relationship is "Do you care enough to do what it takes"? Love does not require a stiff penis, or a supple vagina love requires that you know your partner so well that you can please them regardless. It's not always about sex either that unasked for a back rub or reaching out to hold their hand the unexpected caress all those things are big parts of loving because they are unmistakable indicators that you CARE. That is the crux of it all because someday we will all get to the point where our sexual capacity becomes diminished but that doesn't mean we can stop expressing that caring concern that is the hallmark of love.

I've often heard the expression that you "Have to work at loving" but if you have the right attitude it will not be a chore but a joyous expression of two people who have grown so close that they really understand each other and accept each other on such a deep level that they would be lost without each other.

Love is the most fabulous thing that humans can do it uses all of our creativity and separates us from all living things on this planet. The cruelest thing you can do to another person is lying to them about love. If you don't feel it, don't say it and for God's sake don't marry someone that you do not love that is beyond terribly cruel. But it seems to happen with regularity and the reasons seems to be legion. My wife once told me that she had never been physically attracted to me but that I made her feel safe.

That is a body blow of the worst kind and telling someone something like that is quite cruel. If you weren't attracted to someone then why the hell did you marry them? That makes no sense and is the setup for the perfect storm of a sexless marriage.

But this happens all the time some marry for money or social advantage others to flee from circumstances they are desperate to leave behind. Some get married because they screwed up and someone got pregnant though that is much less common than it once was. After living with someone who rejects you for so long your self-image and confidence hit the sub-basement, and in turn, many people let this chain them down because they become afraid to start over. It can be tough to rebuild your life from scratch but consider this by the time you get to that point you should have a very good idea of what you want and you should have some notion of how to get it.

# Chapter 12.  Setting Ourselves Free

Sexless marriages are just one of many problems that people are facing in what seems to be an ever more egocentric and isolating kind of world. If you are married and have sex less than once a month you are living in a fundamentally sexless marriage, this seems to be an agreed on a definition, and for this discussion, it will work. The numbers of sexless marriages can never truly be known because many people would rather be crucified naked in public than reveal that kind of information but even based on evidence from doctors and psychologists and others involved in the treatment of these problems the numbers are staggering.

There have always been sexless marriages, there is no question of that, and in certain eras of human history, it was even encouraged. But there was also a big disconnect in the way things were handled. The Victorians encouraged women to have their children and then have sex as what was referred to as the wife's duties. That kind of attitude made it almost a certainty that the sex wasn't enjoyable because the woman would lie there and do her duty, which is a sorry excuse for sex. As society evolved the idea of romantic love and other what we see as love practices came into our lexicon of the way things should be. There is always change, and our ideas about sex are no exception, but sometimes the ideas haven't changed enough as we have changed to create a climate for people to be satisfied with their sexual relationships.

Sadly we have often loaded ourselves down with chains and excessively primitive ideas that in our present social structure almost guarantee that there will be many unhappy people. The divorce rate and the numbers of sexless marriages prove this beyond any doubt. Many factors add to our misery, and most of them are self-induced because we have locked ourselves into traditions and ideas that simply don't fit the reality of our situation.

In the last one hundred years, our society has undergone huge upheavals due to industrialization, advances in medicine and technology. We live longer and healthier lives, which changes the dynamic of what is possible for relationships. While there has always been some experimentation around the edges, most people still subscribe to the idea of letting religious practices dictate their relationship practices, but the template being used is well over a thousand years old.

Analysis of these practices brings to light some rather disturbing ideas. The first and primary concern of these rules is that women are owned and when they marry a man he owns their sexuality. It's supposed to go both ways, but our social structure has always seemed to be biased in favor of letting males do about anything they wanted while the wife was pretty much under lock and key. This notorious double standard has been in practice for a very long time, and it allowed men to make rules that allowed them to do things like having concubines, visit prostitutes, have multiple wives and even easily set their wife aside. After all in some cultures even today a man can divorce his wife simply by saying in public three times I divorce thee, I divorce thee, I divorce thee.

The men loaded the dice in the mating game, but that has never stopped those that were determined to bend or break the rules. One of the primary purposes of marriage was to control the inheritance of property. The heirs were incredibly important to a family and men jealously guarded the sexuality of their wife to ensure that the heir was of their bloodline. In effect, a wife was breeding stock and in many cases was treated as such. Keeping control of the land and the goods that the family owned was of paramount importance, and the marriage customs were developed to aid and abet this imperative. There was little concern for romance or happiness or mutual satisfaction with the marriage in most cases it was often a business deal where a marriage occurred to cement alliances and to increase material wealth.

This doesn't mean that romance and concern for the happiness of a mate didn't exist, but it was far outweighed by marriages that were for convenience and financial gain. As our society has become more complex and the average person became more affluent and had more leisure to engage in pursuits other than just surviving our ideas about what our relationships should provide for us underwent many changes but unfortunately the rules from the bad old days of marriage stayed firmly locked in place. Though slight variations occur, marriage is still primarily about owning your partners sexual reproductive capacity to the exclusion of all others.

That doesn't mean that everything is all tidy and orderly, some recent technology that makes it fairly easy to determine genetic parentage of children suggests that somewhere around 5 percent of men are unknowingly raising children that they didn't father. That means that the wife got pregnant elsewhere then let her husband believe the child was his.

The issue here is tied into that ownership idea, and if we cling to this, we are simply setting ourselves up for catastrophic failure of the system of marriage. Actually with the divorce rate being what it is the meltdown seems to have already started. Since we live much longer these days, the idea of being married for life simply seems unrealistic for most people. Facing as much as eighty years with the same person is a much more serious commitment that it was when people only lived to an average age of forty-seven. In our society people now have opportunities to have multiple careers and to do complete transformations of their lives as they follow their interests, which seem to change rapidly. It's unreasonable to expect a rigid institution such as marriage to survive in that environment without some bedrock changes that make marriage more user-friendly to everyone involved. The present system almost guarantees misery for large numbers of people for many reasons.

The average new marriage seems to only last about eight years these days, and serial marriages are very common. This indicates that our expectations of what marriage is and can provide for us are out of line with reality. In this case, it looks like advertising and soap operas are doing us a huge disservice by building up false ideas of what marriage is. The advertising community wants to sell those fancy dresses, big diamond rings, and a multitude of other things that they have tried to make indispensable for the modern bride who feels entitled to all this because she believes that this is what she should get, after all, she saw all those women on television getting all that stuff. I know one woman who has a collection of 7 big diamond engagement rings from her serial marriages which usually seem to last about 2 to 3 years before she jumps ship for another boat she says that's her retirement fund.

Then the misery is further compounded because the young couples with usually very modest incomes assume a huge debt load to buy that house with five bedrooms, three baths, in a nice neighborhood as well as two nice cars, maybe a boat and some nice furniture and all the other trappings that we believe we must have. They want to have it all because they have been conditioned to want it all.

The reality is that all that stuff is usually acquired over a lifetime and is at the end stage of a successful career it's not realistic to expect to begin at the top, but our society pushes this idea relentlessly. We are bombarded every day with the information that if we get this new car or that beautiful home or this fabulous jewelry that it will make us blissfully happy. Sorry, it just doesn't work that way; the majority of people cannot buy those things without going into debt. The statistics don't lie in this case, young people are getting married and assuming a crushing debt load which is assuredly a recipe for disaster.

Having that kind of pressure on them rapidly takes all the fun out of a relationship, and it's normally not very long before the combat over finances begins. It's stressful to be living in a fabulous house and trying to keep up the appearance of success while you are eating hot dogs and ramen because all your income is being used to pay bills and even worse many people end up having to go further into debt to get the hot dogs. The children appear, and the downward spiral continues, more debt, more stress and eventually the wheels come off.

The fastest growing segment of poor people in America is children from homes where there has been a divorce. In these modern times, a divorce often means a division of debts more than a division of assets because the assets are all encumbered by debt. This situation means that instead of a family living in a nice home teetering on the edge of financial disaster there are now two households that have fallen over the edge into poverty. Add to this men and women who run from the responsibility of taking care of their children, and we have created a system that is a disaster area for everyone involved.

Some marriages do succeed the huge numbers of people that get married guarantee there will be some successes, but there are far too many failures to believe that this is a workable system. The emotional damage is enormous, financially it is a disaster of epic proportions, children are perhaps the most damaged of all because they receive the effects not only of divorce induced poverty but the damage that comes with never seeing a successful relationship to model for their future behavior. Each successive generation that survives this trauma and manages to reproduce perpetuates behaviors and attitudes that assure that the damage field will increase in size and complexity.

Sexless marriages can be the result of many factors, but the main issue seems to be a complete incompatibility in the participant's expectations of what marriage should be. The usual pattern is that two people fall in love and while they have the entire boatload of feel good chemistry going on in their brain they seem to each other to be compatible. They may be having sex, which seems to be suitable for a married relationship others because of inhibitions decide to wait until they get married to participate. The problem is that this isn't the way married sex is going to be once they get married and that chemistry assumes more normal levels.

The usual scenario is that the two people involved have different ideas of what marriage is supposed to be. Most of the time in a marriage that is potentially sexless one partner feels that sex is a very low priority and things like work, finances, recreational activities, kids, and accumulating resources should be the main focus of their lives. While the other person thought they were going to get a relationship where intimacy, feeling, and sex would be very high priority items in the marriage. These two opposing ideas of what the marriage should often result in an emotional meltdown as one partner is denied what they feel that they are entitled to in the marriage. Many times it results in a quick divorce and if the participants are lucky they divorce before they have children.

The worst situation is where this takes a few years to become apparent, and there are children, and the debt load and accumulation of things have placed the people in a position where the divorce will result in chaos and even financial disaster. In this case, a sexless marriage may go on for many years causing great pain for the partner who expected emotion, intimacy and a loving relationship because all they ended up with was a roommate or a business partner. This basic incompatibility takes its toll over the long term and can severely damage the partner who needs loving interaction to help them be a happy, well-adjusted person.

The success rate for turning this situation around and making an environment where both partners can thrive is virtually nonexistent; unhappily the majority of the time the only real solution is divorce because in most cases there is not enough common ground to allow a compromise that is acceptable to both partners to be reached. Often the person who sees sex as unnecessary is very inflexible and has no interest in the emotional well-being of their partner, and often they seem to want to treat their mate as an ownership rather than as a person who has feelings and needs. Often these people have other problems that contribute to the destruction of the relationship.

Some of these problems can be explained by psychological disorders of various sorts, but the main problem seems to be just the basic personality types of the people involved. Finding a mate these days is still just about as much of a crapshoot as it has always been. We get an initial attraction going and then when that brain chemistry kicks in we are at the mercy of hormones and chemicals that are designed for one thing, which is to prepare us to breed and make more people.

We share that with every other animal on this planet and though we like to think that our large brains make us invulnerable to that kind of imperative we are dead wrong. The problem is that we have evolved to be much more

72

complex individuals than this primitive reproductive chemistry can allow for. There is no chemical or hormone in there that help us with finding the right person for a longer relationship and since we now live much longer than it takes to reproduce there is a lot of time that we want to fill in with what we call relationships.

There are many different types of relationships, but to be satisfactory to the people involved there must always be compromises made that allow the participants to find some positive things in the relationship. Trying to live in a relationship where one person controls everything or where there is no sharing of responsibility for each other's well-being is extremely destructive. In this sense that relationship has devolved from a partnership to a dictatorship and it will eventually build up a huge amount of resentment because this is abuse plain and simple, it shows a lack of sympathy as well as neglect of the responsibilities that we assume when we enter into the binding relationship contract we call marriage.

Successful marriages have some things in common, to be successful the partners must communicate, they must be engaged and have compassion for their partners feelings, they must be willing to give to the relationship as well as take it, both partners must have a sense that the relationship is about working together toward things that can help both partners be happy. Without these bonds, the marriage is often just an empty shell that two people are pretending happiness in just to project an image of success. The reality is usually either misery for both parties and a disconnected lifestyle where one partner is getting what they need at the expense of the other person. Building a satisfactory relationship is not an easy undertaking nor is it something that can be accomplished quickly. It takes planning, perseverance, compassion and most of all a genuine love and concern for your partner's happiness.

Eventually, it seems that we will have to start changing the fundamental ideas that we have about marriages and relationships to allow for more flexibility and to make allowances so that everyone involved gets a fair share of the good things that love makes possible for us. We need to get away from the idea of ownership; every person is entitled equally to the pursuit of happiness it's in our Constitution and marriage does not supersede this. It is a basic human right that many people seem to think is unimportant as long as they are getting things to go their way. This is critical to our development of a system that is equitable for all.

Our body belongs to us, and we have the right to choose whom we share it with, this is our most intimate possession and can never be owned by someone else. When a refuser decides they will no longer participate in the relationship, they are ignoring all of the promises they made when they married. There is no such thing as adultery or cheating because we cannot own each other. All relationships are negotiable, and all details are only the concern of those directly involved. What consenting adults want to do in their own home or in private is their business and no one else's. Children are a priority responsibility, and there must be a support system in place to make sure that their needs are met. Our society must make sure that all children are taught about their bodies and how to keep themselves safe and healthy. Birth control should be available to all persons. Sexual diseases should be tracked down relentlessly and extinguished.

All of these things will meet with resistance from people who feel they have the right to dictate what other people can do but we must overcome this tendency to truly set ourselves free and allow true equality for all to build relationships in the manner that they are comfortable with. This is our responsibility to offer all the opportunity to pursue life, liberty, and happiness. It is time to remove the law from our relationships with the prudish ignorance established by people from the past.

The present system allows and even encourages abuse, and it must change. Finding the courage and the will to do this may be difficult, but in the long run, the results of not changing can only be tragedy and misery for more people. We must be free to go where our spirit takes us and to love whom we will without others being able to dictate what is supposedly right or wrong. In this case, a simple idea such as being responsible for ourselves and resolving to do no harm to others should be enough to finally offer us the freedom that our intelligence should have given us long ago.

Only those that wanted power over us and have sought to control us stand in the way of true human emancipation at last. It may be a bitter fight against those that are used to dominating us and forcing conformity to their sick ideas, but this battle is one we must win not only for ourselves but for the future to assure that our children can build their lives as they see fit as they find their vision. Throwing off the chains of the dead past offers us the unprecedented opportunity to become much better than we are and to extend the chance to achieve better lives to all. Who can know how this will all end up but the prognosis isn't good as more and more people become isolated in their little worlds and lack social skills as well as any social consciousness about what they do and who they do it too. It's hard to see the future, but it is becoming apparent that people are not as interested in marriage as they once were.

Cohabitation is very common, and many children are born from these unwed relationships. This is a bad situation for children because since there was no marriage getting child support can be problematical because it has to be proven whose children they are in court and often some parents flee to escape paying. In this situation, it makes sense not to have any children simply because there is no commitment to raising them. But people still lack brains enough to do the right thing, and the human race will continue to suffer.

# Chapter 13. Secrets of Self Destruction

Much of the damage that is done by a sexless marriage is self -inflicted. It has its roots in our rejection by our sexless partners, but essentially we are doing bad things to ourselves. We get married and are full of hope that we can build a relationship that will satisfy our needs for many things such as companionship, sex, children, and intimacy. In the beginning, the relationship is fueled by feel good hormones and brain chemicals that kind of equate to the high you would get from other drugs, but these are built in. We are optimistic and are seeing the world through rose-colored glasses. It's not long before reality begins to take hold and suddenly we have bills, jobs, housework, kids and a ton of other things to deal with. All of these things and more create stress, which we have all had before but marriage seems to multiply the stresses, and it can be overwhelming. Nature has provided us with a great stress reliever called sex, but oddly enough the great enemy of sex is stress. The more stressed you get, the more likely you are not to feel interested in sex. Given high enough levels of stress, both men and women can lose all desire for sex. It seems that when the levels of stress reach a certain point that our bodies go into fight or flight mode which is a survival strategy to either get you away from the stress or get you ready for physical combat.

We all find ways to cope with stress; some people hit the refrigerator and comfort themselves with food. Each of these behaviors can create more stress because we often become addicted to these forms of stress relief. Sadly each of these behaviors can contribute to the demise of sex in a marriage. Worse still the loss of sex further erodes the relationship that can create a vicious cycle that continually feeds on itself. As the stress builds the relationship suffers, and each person begins to feel isolated from the other, which further complicates the issue.

As the relationship begins to self -destruct in many cases so do we, our self- esteem is damaged, and we start having doubts about our partners, our relationship and ourselves. Instead of drawing closer together to strengthen the bonds of the relationship we often start retreating and isolating ourselves from our partner. Some people resort to masturbation and porn, some read romance novels, and others retreat into the world of television. Many become workaholics because they would rather be working than deal with the situation at home.

In today's world, many people are spending a lot of time involved in online sex. Cybersex is easily available twenty-four hours a day, and since there is no requirement to have another human present, it is open to everyone. For those that are unlikely to attract a partner it may be a solution that allows them participation in sex, but for others, it has become a substitute for human interaction. It is just as susceptible to abuse as anything else when done to excess. It also seems to be addictive to some people that have difficulty interacting with other people and sometimes becomes their preferred method of sexual expression.

Poor communication skills in any of these environments can be the stroke that kills the relationship. Many of us fall into the trap of expecting our partner to be able to read our mind, but that's never going to happen. There has to be constant communication and feedback going on to allow the two people in the marriage to work together to achieve common goals. If either partner shuts down this vital link, then chaos will surely follow. In a way, most of us start married life full of ideas about how things will be without any real knowledge of what's about to happen. Living in close quarters with someone is entirely different than dating, and even if the couple has lived together for a while, the marriage changes things significantly. When you have been married for a while, and the newness had worn off all of a sudden we start noticing irritating behaviors in our spouses that didn't seem to matter when our brains were flooded with those hormones. The white knight's armor is suddenly rusty, and the fair maiden loses the grace that our imagination may have given her. The reality of marriage sets in if children are added to the mix then the spear is driven home. We find that the reality doesn't match up with our expectations.

Usually, we are never really warned what to expect, and this sudden awakening can come as quite a shock. If there is good communication and a true partnership has been established most marriages will survive this initial smack down. Some crumble because there is no solid connection to keep them together. In some cases, though this initial disappointment starts a downhill slide in the marriage and without good communications skills, the partners may begin to feel as if they are isolated. This feeling of being alone often manifests itself in some behavior that compensates for the loss of close contact with the spouse. Some people turn to drugs or alcohol others find comfort in the refrigerator; sometimes one or the other partner will have an affair. The behaviors are unpredictable because everyone has their way to seek comfort.

Sadly these behaviors aggravate the problem because they can drive the couple even further apart. Many divorces happen at this point, the average new marriage these days only lasts eight years or less. That seems to be about the length of time that people are willing to tolerate the pain of isolation and the feeling of disconnection that occurs when there is a lack of communication. Some marriages beat the odds, and they do have some things in common. Marriages that last are based on good communications and a willingness to engage their partner instead of pulling away when things get difficult. The other long lasting marriage is of the type where one partner gives up and just decides to shut up about their needs and soldier on.

We have all heard the phrase "I needed him/her to be there for me, " and that sums up the critical part of what makes a marriage strong and flexible enough to survive. You must be engaged with your partner, which means sharing the good things as well as the bad. This is intimacy in its most crucial form. Without intimacy, there may be a living arrangement with two people sharing a home, but the ability to share our lives with each other is what makes a marriage a thing that both partners can cherish. This is no easy task, and apparently, it is beyond the ability of many people to achieve. There are so many fractured relationships among us that a solid marriage with two people that can function together is becoming increasingly rare. There are huge numbers of people limping along in marriages where neither partner is really happy about the situation for various reasons. Many of these people have become estranged from each other emotionally as well as physically. They struggle to maintain the appearance of normality when their marriage is anything but normal or at least what is usually defined as normal.

In many cases, these marriages are beyond redemption because the two people have pushed each other so far away that there is no longer any love or concern for each other. In some cases, one partner has assumed control of the relationship and is attempting to manipulate their partner. This behavior may be subtle but as time passes it usually becomes much more obvious. Many of these relationships last for years because one of the participants is what is called co- dependent.

Co -dependency seems to come in many gradations from someone that is a people pleaser that likes to be helpful for the positive attention they get from it to the doormat spouse or lover that is in the clutches of a passive aggressive spouse who uses them and emotionally abuses them. The important issue is how much they are willing to accept before they will finally say enough; I must do something about this. Many co-dependents never free themselves and remain in abusive situations because they simply are addicted to that type of relationship.

Co -dependency is described as a tendency to be very passive and overly concerned with taking care of the needs of others with a little concern for the consequences to themselves. This type of dependency can occur in almost any type of relationship; it is often visible as denial of obvious facts, repressed anger, low self-esteem, excessive passivity and letting others control them. Co- dependency is described as an extreme situation where these types of behaviors are exaggerated. Co-dependency can lead to other self-destructive behaviors like abusing alcohol and drugs, anorexia or bulimia, sex addiction (with other people of course), excessive dependence on religion, and many other problems.

Co -dependents are frequently addicted to hope; they hope that the person that they have fastened on to as their shining star will change. Anyone that is involved in a serious relationship has some level of co-dependency; this is the nature of an interactive relationship that has some level of intimacy. But here we are talking about a more extreme unhealthy version of this relationship that can create multiple problems not only for the co-dependent but can also be passed on to their children. This is a learned behavior, it is not a disease, but nonetheless, it can do terrible damage to the people involved in the co- dependent relationship as well as those on the periphery.

Co -dependency often originates in childhood; feelings of being neglected or emotionally abandoned by parents can cause the child not to have coping skills or normal levels of self-esteem. They become emotionally isolated and have issues with trusting others and even in trusting their thoughts and feelings. To make themselves feel better codependents will usually settle into a pattern of behavior that makes them feel better, this can be alcohol, drugs, gambling, excessive dependence on religion, food, sex or whatever thing that they have taught themselves will ease the emotional pain. They often become addicted to relationships and will go to extraordinary lengths to hang on to them. They have a fear of being abandoned that often immobilizes them in unhealthy relationships far past the time when it should have ended.

All of this may sound familiar because many co-dependents are also passive aggressive. So when you pair up a co-dependent with a hardcore passive aggressive, there may be a subtle struggle for control. A passive aggressive co- dependent relationship isn't going to help either person because eventually, one partner will become dominant due to their desire to control the partnership. The weaker partner will become the subordinate doormat for the marriage.

In choosing partners co -dependents can be their own worst enemy because they choose someone that fits the pattern that they are familiar with. Often they will choose someone that is passive aggressive because it fits with what they have become accustomed to in previous relationships. This is the main reason that women who are abused often end up choosing someone else that will abuse them. It's very hard to break this cycle without help because the co-dependent can't recognize that they are behaving this way. The co-dependent gives up the power in a relationship to their dominant partner and suffers in silence. This power imbalance causes distress for the co-dependent, but the thought of giving up the relationship terrifies them even more.

A person that is co -dependent is almost always deeply depressed by their situation because they cannot see any way to move out of the pattern. This depression will affect all areas of their lives and often further aggravate an already difficult situation. It is an insidious problem that unfortunately can be passed on to their children. Since this is a learned behavior child often imitate the methods of handling relationships that are demonstrated to them. Children of co-dependent people often end up as co-dependents too furthering the misery and carrying into their relationships the seeds of their destruction.

Some indicators can help determine if a person is codependent:

1) A codependent person is often more tuned into someone else's reality than their own. They love to fix things for other people, but their motivation is that it makes them feel good which, is their payoff for doing well. Co-dependents expect a return on their investment when they do something this often is an expectation that the person that they have helped will give them some form of control over them. They seem to think that doing something for you entitles them to tell you what to do with your life.

2) Co-dependent people are often obsessed with other people's pain. They use this as an excuse to interfere with the sufferer's life; they particularly like to perform self-sacrificial acts. This is like empathy gone wild where the co- dependent may feel more pain than the person who owns the problem.

3) Usually, co-dependents are extremely needy people; they want their object of co-dependence under their watchful eye all the time. They frequently check up on their partners and will get in the way to prevent relationships with other people. Their objective is to focus all attention on themselves. They frequently ask questions like 'Do you still love me" or

"Will you always be there for me," it's a miserable existence for the person that is in the co-dependent person's sights.

4) Many co-dependents are workaholics; they feel the need for approval to be so critical that they will do virtually anything to achieve what they see as the reward for their obsessive dedication. They do more than their share all the time because it is a way of demanding attention and approval. They will often act like martyrs using the extra work as an excuse to ignore their families.

5) The constant need for approval and recognition is a hint that there is co- dependency involved. But only when it carried to extremes, most people enjoy being recognized for achievement, but co-dependents practice it as a crutch for their low self-esteem. It's almost impossible for a true co-dependent to have any love for their self, they do not think they are worthy of love or that others care about them. Many times people that are co-dependent will never believe that someone who says that they love them doesn't have some ulterior motive for saying it. They do not have a strong sense of self and if you ask them who they are men will often respond with either their job title and women often respond with their place in a relationship such as a wife or a mother.

6) During childhood, co-dependents have felt as though they were abandoned and it is one of their primary fears. This fear creates a situation that makes a co- dependent lack skill in forming healthy bonds with other people. They have a difficult time showing feelings and often feel unable to have a difference of opinion with another person. In a nutshell, co-dependent people feel terrible about themselves and can't believe that anyone would ever want them. This lack of a clear sense of self can make them very vulnerable to other manipulative personality types who seem to seek this type of person because they are easily dominated.

Co -dependents often have huge amounts of suppressed anger simmering below the surface, and it is often directed at their selves even though there is no reason for self-punishment. Their feelings of self-worth are so badly damaged that they find it inconceivable that someone could love them just as they are. The result is that a co-dependent person wears a mask much of the time and they hide behind being over achievers and do-gooders. They rely heavily on their works to prove their worth even though they don't believe that they are worthy of anything. This is a sad way for a person to live but there is hope. Co-dependent people can recover with proper guidance. It's not an easy process, but there have been fair amounts of success with helping people overcome these issues and going on to live better and happier lives.

# Chapter 14.  Madonna/Whore Complex

This is something that is talked about sometimes, but few people seem to know what this is about or what effects it might have on people. There is a debate about whether this condition exists or not but for the sake of information it should at least be mentioned.

Madonna /Whore Complex is a male condition where a man refuses to have sex with his wife to preserve her purity in his mind. He will have sex with other women because he sees them as whores who are dirty and are to be used as sex objects. He divides all women into two categories the Madonna (the pure women) and the whores who are everyone else. This type of man views sex as dirty and something that he should only do with whores. This doesn't mean he doesn't like sex men of this type are usually very sexually active but never with their wives or someone they are considering having a long-term relationship with. If he is dating a woman and she gives in to his sexual advances she has labeled herself as a whore in his eyes, and he will have sex with her, but he will never consider a long-term relationship with her.

Men that have this problem will frequently marry a woman and then soon after the marriage or after a child is born will quit having sex with her because she must stay pure to be worthy of his affection. Then he turns to the whores for his sexual satisfaction and should the wife try to get him to have sex with her by trying to be seductive she runs the risk of also being classified as unworthy of his affection and categorized as a whore. It is critical to this man that his wife be a virgin before marriage this is the ultimate sign of her "goodness" He will often test her by trying to get her to give in to his sexual overtures and if she does she is immediately classified as a whore and is discarded as a potential mate.

There are several theories as to what causes this condition; some psychiatrists believe it is caused by unmet needs for intimacy that he experienced as an infant. They theorize that he may unconsciously seek out a woman who reminds him of his mother in an attempt to finally meet those needs that were missing in his infancy. When he marries it must be a "good" woman whose virginity was intact when they began dating, untainted by any previous sexual experience.

If she passes all of his purity tests she may be loved, protected and treasured but she will never again be offered a sexual relationship. She will often be emotionally and verbally abused as she attempts to get her husband to be intimate with her. The man considers her to be pure and in his mind, he cannot dirty her by having sex with her and damaging her purity.

At first, a woman who falls in love with a Madonna/Whore man may be thrilled by his placing her on a pedestal and showing such concern for her well-being. Eventually, this worship becomes a prison as she matures, his expectation is that she must abstain from all of that "dirty" sex and maintain her purity. When he is courting her, he may have been quite passionate and overwhelming for someone who is sexually naive. Then once they marry, she might believe her husband has lost interest in her because of her innocence, which she may attempt to remedy by trying to turn him on with sexy clothing or provocative actions. This will usually backfire and cause him to accuse her of acting like a whore and criticizing her by telling her she is stupid and acting whorish.

A normal woman, even if she is brought up in a strictly religious home where good girls don't, believes that once she is married, then it's time to commence sexual love. With a Madonna Whore man, she is doomed to an essentially sexless marriage, there may be enough sexual appointments to start a family but with a child or children the sexual distance often increases, and the marriage becomes completely sexless. Once she becomes a mother, he sees her as someone that should not be "defiled" by sex.

A man who has this condition sees it as proper for him to have sex with whores, so infidelity is usually a way of life for him. In his mind, any woman who succumbs to his advances is only a whore and as such is used as a sex object. On the other hand, he may be extremely jealous of his wife and will often be extremely controlling. In his mind she may be tempted anytime, she is out of his sight, and he will believe she's an easy target for any man that shows a desire for her. Even though he may be the only one who is cheating on his marriage in his mind, it's only a matter of time until his wife goes from a Madonna to becoming a whore.

This problem is hard to spot because his dysfunctional views may be camouflaged by his suave ladies' man approach to women. It appears that this condition is a form of obsessive-compulsive behavior and this should be dealt with by a mental health professional. Any woman unlucky enough to get into a relationship with a Madonna Whore man is in for a very bad time indeed. Being married to a man that cheats, doesn't want you to be sexual in any way, is very jealous and controlling, and wants you to remain locked into a sexless marriage is a sure recipe for unhappiness.

If as a woman you find yourself involved in this sort of relationship seek help wherever you can find it. It may be possible to break this cycle with the help of a trained professional.

# Chapter 15. Pornography

The idea of sexually explicit drawings has been around since caveman days. Throughout history, there have always been various attempts at creating erotic images, but in recent history, we have managed to create media where we can watch real people doing every kind of sex act possible. Pornography is a big business taking in billions of dollars each year worldwide. Some countries have tried to restrict it at times it has been banned but what it has never been being stopped. Some types of pornography such as those that exploit children are almost universally illegal, (personally I think these people should be locked up forever with choice bits of their anatomy removed) but in many cases, there are many avenues around the law, so this continues to flourish.

For a lot of people the idea of pornography is tied to magazines and pictures, and up until fairly recently, that was the case. But as soon as someone invented the motion picture guess what was on the screen. As humans, we all have an interest in sex if we are normally adjusted and healthy. The idea of two lovers watching a pornographic film together doesn't upset most people's ideas of permissible behavior. It seems though that individual's use pornography most often as a means of generating excitement while they masturbate and even that might not generate much angst among most people.

It has even become fashionable among some armchair non-professionals to talk about porn addiction. This is not recognized as an addiction by the professional mental health community yet but has become a way to label people that overuse pornography, which may be changing as this becomes a bigger problem, and more people turn to the mental health community for help and answers. This overuse has some serious drawbacks; it has caused people to lose their jobs, caused divorces, and played havoc with the abuser's life. While not technically an addiction yet many of the features closely resemble addictive behavior.

Men are much more likely to abuse pornography and since the internet has made porn just a mouse click away many young men and older men without a sex partner have become fascinated by the variety of easily available and often free pornography available online. People that use online porn often spend large amounts of time alone with their computer masturbating to online porn. This behavior can become almost obsessive and detrimental to the abuser's life.

Within recent times doctors have been seeing increasing numbers of people that are impotent with their mates due to over exposure to pornography. It seems that the over stimulation of continued use of pornography sets the arousal threshold so high in these individuals that they can no longer become aroused by their sex partner. This behavior has become much more common as broadband Internet has made it so easy to obtain access to these materials.

Humans have always been obsessed with sex and the drive to reproduce hard wired into us and the visual signals generated by pornography stimulate us sexually. Men and women both can get hooked on the anonymous thrills available through Internet porn. Web cams let people see each other and allow people to perform sexual acts for others while still being in the privacy of their own home. If this behavior becomes obsessive, it can create havoc in the addict's life causing them to withdraw from friends and family and sometimes lose their jobs as well. This can be a serious problem for some people. When a man or woman chooses Internet porn over their spouse, they have a real problem, and if they refuse to seek help, the chances are that their spouse will end up leaving them behind at some point.

The next level of disengagement for people is on its way, even now some companies make life like dolls that replicate humans that are used for sexual purposes. The next generation will be the so-called sexbots, which will be robotic sex partners. There is already interest in this, and several companies are working on developing more realistic mechanical sex partners ever. Everybody is fairly familiar with sex toys, the vibrator has been around for decades, and the sex toy industry is huge as is the pornography industry.

Sex is of interest to almost every healthy human in some form. The idea of using toys for pleasure as a couple or alone has lost the stigma once attached to such behavior and now is considered a normal outlet for couples seeking variety as well as for people that don't have a sex partner. The thing that I find threatening about dolls and sexbots is that it removes the idea of two people having a sexual relationship. Using a mechanical mechanism as a substitute for human interaction dehumanizes people and creates people that are isolated from others. This kind of isolation doesn't provide social stimulation and the humanizing effect of having relationships with other people. This looks very much like something that could aggravate mental illness or maybe even facilitate its development.

People have been moving in this direction for quite some time as more and more of our activities become solo pursuits such as video gaming, watching television and spending hours alone with the Internet. Some schools are trying to discontinue the practice of giving children recess where they can interact with other children. I feel this is crucial to developing social skills and normal interactive behavior. As time passes many people are becoming less socially active and fail to develop adequate social skills, we are seeing one of the results of this in the inability of people to develop satisfying personal relationships.

These days most people have a huge number of acquaintances with cell phones full of numbers and gazillions of Face book friends, but for many, the numbers of real people that they come into face-to-face contact with is rapidly shrinking. These trends seem to point toward a day in the future when people will no longer be interested in having meat people friends. They will get their interaction through the wizardry of electronic media and no longer require others as friends or mates.

It may seem far-fetched, and in a way, it is because I think there will always be significant numbers of people that treasure their families and friends. They will always be interested in having warm human interaction relationships. But for those others, we may be looking at the beginnings of the development of a human type that has no needs for others at all. Those people worry me because this bunch will lack empathy and most other traits that we expect humans to have. Without socialization, these people will lack the concepts that we learn from interacting with others such as the concept of right and wrong essentially they may become sociopaths without consciences. We have people like that now we call them serial killers.

It is pretty sad to imagine how empty someone must feel that they make love to an inanimate object. They will never feel loved at all, and that seems so terrible that it is hard to comprehend what that could do to a person. But people are cruel, and manners have degenerated a lot being rude, crude and socially unacceptable seems to be the fashion these days. But social skills are becoming a rare thing to possess in a world that encourages isolation with all the solo activities such as watching TV playing computer games and other isolating activities. I sometimes wonder if eventually, we will all go extinct because everyone is sitting in front of their TV alone and no one knows how to interact with another person enough to perpetuate the species.

# Conclusion

Sex in a Passive Aggressive Marriage can be a confusing and hurtful topic to discuss as it digs deep into our emotional core. Sex is a way of building intimacy between partners, of meeting emotional needs that we all have. A "sexless marriage" causes a range of harmful effects from resentment, low self-esteem, to distrust; all stemming from the fact that your partner is not meeting your emotional and physical needs, and this happens with no negotiation or previous agreement including your needs' consideration. This is the fastest path either to divorce or chronic frustration.

Everyone's needs for love and connection are the same, but we seek to fulfill needs in different ways, according to our attachment styles. When two partners have different attachment styles, they can be mismatched in their methods of needs fulfillment, causing stress, hurt and confusion. We now know that withholding of sex by a passive aggressive partner is, beyond being his only method of communication available, also the tool he uses to control the emotional bond of intimacy between himself and you, his spouse, because of his avoidant attachment style learned as a child. He is afraid of close emotional connections and the risk of feeling trapped and getting hurt, so he pushes and pulls at the ties between you two, attempting to get his emotional needs met (some company) while keeping this "safe" distance (not so "demanding" company).

Discovering that you are married to someone with whom your needs and attachment styles are mismatched can be very challenging, and create a sense of loss and grief over "losing" or letting go of the "ideal mate" you were in love with when you got married.

This discovery brings about the need to decide if you are going to stay in your marriage and work with the man you are married to (rather than fighting to maintain the illusion of the one you thought you were married to) or let go of the marriage altogether. But both options hold hope that you will find happiness and fulfillment in your future, now that you know the true nature of your emotional needs, which are not easily canceled out or forgettable.

If you decide to stay in your marriage, you will need to readjust your view of your partner. Change your perception that they are a rejecting person, "a jerk" , unfeeling, etc., and accept that although their methods are not good enough, they are the best that they right now. If you can let go of some of your anger and hurt, and forgive the circumstances that made them an expert in avoidance, you  may be able to find hope in your partner and your marriage and move forward in working with the reality of them towards a better relationship between you.

Understanding the needs of both partners and  knowing about the strong influence of your attachment styles will go a long way towards satisfying those needs addressed and fulfilled for both partners, creating more balance and harmony, happier sex, and a more secure attachment.

Printed in Great Britain
by Amazon

59245113R00058